# Secretary's Modern Guide to English Usage

## Jean C. Vermes

Parker Publishing Company, Inc.
West Nyack, New York

© 1981, by

PARKER PUBLISHING COMPANY, INC.

West Nyack, New York

Library of Congress Cataloging in Publication Data

Vermes, Jean Campbell Pattison.
  Secretary's modern guide to English usage.

  Includes index.
  1.  English language—Grammar—1950-
2.  English language—Usage.   3.   Secretaries—Hand-
books, manuals, etc.   I.   Title.
PE1112.V43        428.2        81-9515
ISBN 0-13-797365-9        AACR2

Printed in the United States of America

# Introduction

Language, written and spoken, is such a vital part of business life that no secretary can afford to neglect its proper use. Your function, like that of a TV commentator or newspaper reporter, is to communicate, and language is the tool of your trade.

English usage is constantly evolving, and this book brings you up to date on the latest developments. In recent years, business practices and terminology have changed so rapidly that many words defined for you here, along with their pronunciation and correct spelling, cannot be found in the average dictionary.

Modern business correspondence is losing its old formality, and you will learn techniques to make your own letters conform to the new trend. You will also be provided with simple rules to solve those annoying little everyday problems, such as when to use **lie** or **lay, who** or **whom, that** or **which,** and how to punctuate for maximum effect.

No matter how accomplished you may think you are in the use of the English language, you will discover you still have more to learn. For example:

**What is wrong with this sentence?**

When a person endorses a check by only signing their name, please instruct them in the correct procedure. (Answer in Chapter 5, item 5:1b.)

**Pronounce and abbreviate the following words:**

Centimeter, kilometer, kilogram, millimeter, milligram. (Answers in Chapter 11, item 11:2; Chapter 10, 10:4f; and Chapter 1, 1:4.)

**If you heard someone make this remark, what would you think it meant?**

The interface between your department and ours is inadequate. (Answer in Chapter 2, item 2:5a.)

This book provides answers to the above questions, plus anything else you may wish to know on the subject of the English language. The table of contents is the basis of a novel FIND-O-MATIC indexing system, in which each subject is keyed by number. The number also appears in the margin of each page of the text. Since every item in the book is identified numerically, there is no need to search endlessly for the exact usage or other information you require. Everything is explained briefly and clearly, so that you understand precisely why you should use a certain word or construction. The text is conveniently divided into three parts, one on spoken English, one on written English, and a third on the visual appearance of the letters you write.

First, there is a section on effective speech, to advise you on your daily use of the language in your conversation with clients and co-workers. Good English speech is an important business asset because careless words can lead to confusion and error, while precise words convey your exact meaning. Diction and pronunciation are also covered here, as well as proven methods of enlarging your vocabulary.

Written English is the subject of the second part of the book, where you can check quickly to make sure of the spelling and punctuation in the letters you transcribe. It will also give you helpful tips on grammatical construction, so that you can compose good letters of your own, or edit those of your employer when necessary.

The third part is concerned with the eye appeal of your letters and memos, and the forms they should take. You can check this section for information on forms of address, letter styles, and word division, items that will make your correspondence as attractive as it is correct.

Everything you need to know on any question is immediately available to you in these pages. For instance, suppose you were unsure of how to pronounce the word **formidable.** You would look in Part I of the contents under the chapter on pronunciation, turn to the indicated paragraph—1:3a, **Words Ending in ABLE**—and there discover that **formidable** is pronounced with the accent on the first syllable: **FOR-midable.**

If your problem involved spelling an unfamiliar word, such as **appurtenances,** you would look in Part II under the chapter on spelling, turn to the indicated item—7:5, **200 Specialized Business Words and Expressions**—and then go through the list until you reached the subject you wanted—7:5g, **Real Estate**—and there you would find your word, **appurtenances.** The six primary rules for spelling in item 7:1 will also help you determine the way to spell many other words that are commonly misspelled.

At the end of each section, there is a special feature consisting of time-saving charts you can reproduce and tack on the wall for instant reference, such as **Pronunciation Reminder, Spelling Tips,** or **Three Handy Rules of Grammar.** You can also make up your own charts with additional answers to problems in each area that you find especially troublesome.

Your command of English goes deeper than correct usage. It is a reflection of your personality and background. The words you use, and the way you express your thoughts, convey an impression that is just as significant as your physical appearance. In this connection, humorist Goodman Ace once declared that a slim beauty he was watching on television said "between my husband and I" instead of "between my husband and me," and immediately, in his estimation, gained eighteen pounds. With this book on your desk, you can watch your language as closely as you watch your figure. You will find the results equally worthwhile.

**Jean C. Vermes**

# Also by the Author

Secretary's Guide to Dealing with People
Complete Book of Business Etiquette

# Contents

## 8

Contents

**PART II**
**Effective Letters**

**Chapter 5   GRAMMAR SIMPLIFIED** .................. **85**

**Chapter 6   QUICK AND EASY PUNCTUATION** ......... **105**

## 12

Contents

# Part 1

# EFFECTIVE SPEECH

# 1. PRONUNCIATION AND ENUNCIATION

First impressions are vitally important, especially for a secretary. In your various business relationships you project an image, not only of yourself, but also of your immediate superior and of your firm as a whole. Associates judge you by your grooming, your clothes, and your speech. No matter how perfect your appearance, you can spoil the entire effect with slurred enunciation and mispronounced words. Everyone gets careless in this respect occasionally, sometimes without being conscious of it.

## 1:1 BE CAREFUL, YOUR DICTION IS SHOWING!

Make it a point to listen to your own speech for just one day. You may be surprised at some of the unattractive locutions you repeatedly use. Watch out particularly for the following:

| Expression | Translation |
|------------|-------------|
| Cancha | Can't you |
| Woncha | Won't you |
| Idonwanna | I don't want to |
| I'm gonna | I am going to |
| I'll meecha | I will meet you |
| Lessgo | Let's go |
| Watchawant | What do you want |

Other contractions that you may find yourself unconsciously using are the dropped **g**'s, in words such as, "doin'," "seein'," and "goin'," as well as "len'th" and "stren'th." Do not, however, try to counteract your slurred speech with exaggerated emphasis. Reclaim the lost consonants, but do not stress them as in "doingh," "seeingh," or "goingh."

Above all, do not sound the **t** in the group of words ending in **sten** or **ften.** The **t**'s should never be sounded in the following:

Fas(t)en

Lis(t)en

Has(t)en

Of(t)en

Sof(t)en

After enunciation comes a more complicated problem, pronunciation. In a country as large as the United States, there are some regional differences in pronunciation. The dictionary itself gives second choices in pronunciation for a number of words. The first choice should always be used unless you are someplace where certain words are pronounced differently and another pronunciation would make you sound snobbish or affected.

## 1:2 THE RADIO ANNOUNCER'S TEST

A number of words that are commonly mispronounced have been gathered into a paragraph that is used on radio as an "announcer's test." Try it and see how well you can score on the bold words before looking at the answers that follow.

The old man with the **flaccid** face and **dour** expression **grimaced** when asked if he were **conversant** with **zoology, mineralogy,** or the **culinary** arts. "Not to be **secretive,**" he said, "I may tell you that I'd given **precedence** to the study of **genealogy.** But since my father's **demise,** it has been my **vagary** to remain **incognito** because of an **inexplicable, lamentable,** and **irreparable** family **schism.** It resulted from a **heinous** crime, committed at our **domicile** by an **impious** scoundrel. To **err** is human ... but this affair was so

**grievous** that only my **inherent acumen** and **consummate** tact saved me."

### Correct Pronunciations

| | |
|---|---|
| flaccid | FLAK-sid |
| dour | DEW-er |
| grimaced | grim-AYCED |
| conversant | CON-versant |
| zoology | ZOE-ology |
| mineralogy | miner-AL-ogy |
| culinary | CUE-linary |
| secretive | se-CREE-tive |
| precedence | pre-SEED-ence |
| genealogy | jeeny-AL-ogy |
| demise | de-MIZE |
| vagary | va-GAY-ry |
| incognito | in-COG-nee-to |
| inexplicable | in-EX-plicable |
| lamentable | LAM-entable |
| irreparable | ir-REP-arable |
| schism | SIZZ-em |
| heinous | HAY-nus |
| domicile | domi-SILE |
| impious | IM-pius |
| err | EHR |
| grievous | GREE-vus |
| inherent | in-HER-ent |
| acumen | a-CUE-men |
| consummate (adjective) | CON-sum-mit |

Counting one point for each word pronounced correctly, a score of 21 to 25 indicates that you only need to consult a dictionary or pronunciation list occasionally. A score of 15 to 20 is good, but you must watch yourself carefully, check when in doubt, and learn a few rules that will help you determine how certain words should be pronounced.

## 1:3 FOUR EASY PRONUNCIATION RULES

Unfortunately, all pronunciation rules have exceptions, but here is a good general guide.

### 1:3a Words Ending in ABLE

Words of more than two syllables ending in **able** are usually accented on the first syllable.

| | |
|---|---|
| AM·icable | FOR·midable |
| AP·plicable | HOS·pitable |
| COM·parable | LAM·entable |
| DES·picable | PREF·erable |
| EX·plicable | REP·utable |
| | REV·ocable |

**Exceptions:** When a prefix is added to any of the above, the accent remains on the originally stressed syllable, which now becomes the second syllable: in-AP·plicable, in-COM·parable, in-EX·plicable, in-HOS·pitable, dis-REP·utable, ir-REV·ocable, ir-REP·arable.

### 1:3b Words Ending in ATE

In words ending in **ate**, the last syllable in the noun or adjective sounds like **it**, while the last syllable of the verb sounds like **ate**.

| | Noun or Adjective | Verb |
|---|---|---|
| advocate | advo·kit | advo·cate |
| alternate | alter·nit | alter·nate |
| articulate | articu·lit | articu·late |
| associate | associ·it | associ·ate |
| consummate | consum·mit | consum·mate |
| degenerate | degener·it | degener·ate |
| delegate | dele·git | dele·gate |
| deliberate | deliber·it | deliber·ate |
| elaborate | elabor·it | elabor·ate |
| estimate | esti·mit | esti·mate |
| graduate | gradu·it | gradu·ate |
| importunate | importu·nit | importu·nate |
| intimate | inti·mit | inti·mate |
| moderate | moder·it | moder·ate |
| precipitate | precipi·tit | precipi·tate |
| separate | sepa·rit | sepa·rate |
| subordinate | subordi·nit | subordi·nate |
| syndicate | syndi·kit | syndi·cate |

**Exceptions:**
**Nouns**
candi-date
concen-trate
de-bate
re-bate
poten-tate

**1:3c** Words Ending in ILE

In words of more than one syllable ending in **ile**, the last syllable is usually pronounced **ill**. (If you have heard English actors pronounce it to rhyme with **smile**, that is because British pronunciation differs from the American in certain respects.)
The following all end in **ill**.

| | |
|---|---|
| agile | mercantile |
| docile | puerile |
| fertile | servile |
| fragile | sterile |
| futile | textile |
| hostile | versatile |
| juvenile | virile |
| *mobile | volatile |

***Mobile**, in some uses, is pronounced "mo-beel."

These exceptions end as in **smile**.

| | |
|---|---|
| compile | exile |
| crocodile | infantile |
| defile | profile |
| *domicile | senile |
| turnstile | |

***Domicile** is sometimes spelled **domicil**, and pronounced like **ill**.

**1:3d** Words Pronounced According to Use

A two-syllable word, used as both noun and verb, is accented on the first syllable for the noun and on the second syllable for the verb.

| Noun | Verb |
|------|------|
| CON-duct | con-DUCT |
| IN-sult | in-SULT |
| PER-fume | per-FUME |
| PROD-uce | pro-DUCE |
| PROG-ress | pro-GRESS |
| REF-use | re-FUSE |

**Exceptions:** **Preface**, **comment**, and **trespass** are accented on the first syllable, whether used as nouns or verbs. **Crusade, decline,** and **dispatch** are all accented on the last syllable, whether used as nouns or verbs.

## 1:4 101 FREQUENTLY MISPRONOUNCED WORDS

A desk dictionary is an essential part of any secretary's equipment for checking spelling and pronunciation when you are in doubt. In many cases, however, you may be mispronouncing without being aware of your mistakes. The following list gives the preferred pronunciation according to Webster's dictionary. Alternate pronunciations are sometimes acceptable, but the preferred one should always be your choice.

**A**

| | |
|------|------|
| abdomen | AB-do-men |
| affluent | AFF-loo-ent |
| appellate | ap-PELL-it |
| athlete | ATH-leet |

**B**

| | |
|------|------|
| bade | BAD |
| beautiful | BYOO-tih-full |
| bicycle | BY-sickle |

**C**

| | |
|------|------|
| chauffeur | show-FUR |
| chiropodist | kih-ROPP-o-dist |
| clandestine | clan-DESS-tin |

**D**

| | |
|------|------|
| dais | DAY-is |
| data, datum | DAY-ta (plural), DAY-tum (singular) |
| divers | DY-verz (several) |
| diverse | dy-VERS (different) |

**E**

| | |
|---|---|
| emeritus | eh-MERR-ih-tus |
| erudite | ERR-yoo-dite |
| exigency | EK-sih-jen-sy |
| exquisite | EKS-kwi-sit |

**F**

| | |
|---|---|
| facetious | fah-SEE-shus |
| February | FEB-roo-erry |
| finance | fih-NANS |
| fracas | FRAY-cus |

**G**

| | |
|---|---|
| gamut | GAMM-ut |
| garage | gah-RAZH |
| gibberish | JIB-er-ish |
| grimace | grih-MAYCE |

**H**

| | |
|---|---|
| harass | HARR-ass |
| hedonism | HEE-don-izm |
| heinous | HAY-nus |
| humble | HUMM-b'l |

**I**

| | |
|---|---|
| implacable | im-PLAY-kah-b'l |
| incognito | in-KOG-nih-to |
| indigent | IN-dih-jent |
| integral | in-TEH-gral |

**J**

| | |
|---|---|
| jocose | jo-COSE |

**K**

| | |
|---|---|
| kiln | KILL |
| kilogram | KILL-o-gram |
| kilometer | KILL-o-meter |
| kimono | kih-MOE-nuh |

**L**

| | |
|---|---|
| largess | LARR-jess |
| larynx | LARR-ingks |
| leisure | LEE-zher |
| lichen | LYE-ken |

**M**

| | |
|---|---|
| marquis | MAHR-kwis |
| methane | METH-ane |

| | |
|---|---|
| morale | mo-RAL |
| morass | mo-RASS |
| mores | MOE-reez |
| mundane | mun-DANE |

**N**

| | |
|---|---|
| nadir | NAY-der |
| naive | nah-EVE |
| naphtha | NAFF-tha |
| nomenclature | NO-men-klay-ture |

**O**

| | |
|---|---|
| obligatory | ah-BLIG-ah-tory |
| ornate | or-NATE |
| overt | OH-vert |

**P**

| | |
|---|---|
| paradigm | PAR-a-dime |
| perjure | PURR-jer |
| prelate | PRELL-it |
| prelude | PRELL-ude |
| prerogative | preh-ROGG-ah-tiv |
| pristine | PRISS-teen |
| propane | PRO-pane |
| pumpkin | PUMP-kin |

**Q**

| | |
|---|---|
| quadruple | KWOD-roo-p'l |
| querulous | KWER-uh-luss |
| quietus | kwy-EE-tuss |
| quinine | KWY-nine |

**R**

| | |
|---|---|
| rapport | rah-PORE |
| rarity | RARR-i-tee |
| recluse | reh-KLOOS |
| redress | reh-DRESS |
| relapse | reh-LAPS |
| requisite | REK-wih-zit |
| respite | RESS-pit |
| romance | ro-MANS |

**S**

| | |
|---|---|
| sadism | SAD-iz'm |

| | |
|---|---|
| salient | SAY-li-ent |
| satyr | SAT-er |
| secretive | seh-KREE-tiv |
| sinecure | SIGH-neh-cure |
| sojourn | so-JURN |
| subtle | SUT'l |

## T

| | |
|---|---|
| teetotaler | tee-TOE-t'ler |
| termagant | TUR-mah-gant |
| thesaurus | theh-SAW-rus |
| trachea | TRAY-key-a |
| trampoline | TRAM-po-linn |
| turbine | TUR-binn |

## U

| | |
|---|---|
| ubiquitous | yew-BIK-wih-tus |
| ultimatum | ul-tih-MAY-tum |
| untoward | un-TOW-erd |

## V

| | |
|---|---|
| vagary | vah-GAR-ee |
| valet | VAL-ett |
| verbatim | vur-BAY-tim |
| virago | vih-RAY-go |

## W

| | |
|---|---|
| wisteria | wis-TIH-ri-a |
| worsted | WOOS-ted |
| wreak | REEK |

## Z

| | |
|---|---|
| zoology | zo-OLL-o-ji |
| zucchini | zoo-KEY-nee |
| zwieback | TSVEE-bak |

## 1:5 SEVEN SECRETS OF CORRECT PRONUNCIATION

Here are seven simple ways to correct common flaws in pronunciation. Once you become aware of them, you will find your diction immeasurably improved.

## 1:5a Sounds That Are Often Omitted

First and most important, you must watch out for slipshod pronunciation that leaves out vowels and consonants intended to be heard, as in **arctic**, which should be pronounced "AHRK-tic," not "AHR-tic." A few samples will illustrate.

|  | Right | Wrong |
|---|---|---|
| artists | AHR-tists | AHR-tis |
| asked | ASKT | AST |
| candidate | KAN-dih-date | KAN-ih-date |
| chocolate | CHOCK-uh-lit | CHAWK-lit |
| diamond | DYE-uh-mund | DYE-mund |
| February | FEB-ru-ary | FEB-u-ary |
| fifth | FIFTH | FITH |
| government | GUV-ern-ment | GUV-er-ment |
| hundred | HUND-red | HUN-red |
| language | LANG-gwij | LANG-wij |
| liable | LYE-a-b'l | LYEb'l |
| library | LYE-bray-ry | LYE-berry |
| quantity | QUAN-tih-ty | QUAN-it-ty |
| recognize | RECK-og-nize | RECK-uh-nize |
| temperature | TEMP-er-uh-cher | TEMP-uh-cher |
| valuable | VAL-u-able | VAL-ub'l |
| veterinary | VET-er-i-neri | VET-ri-neri |

## 1:5b Sounds That Are Unnecessary

Another careless speech habit is the addition of sounds that do not belong. Saying "ATH-a-lete" instead of "ATH-lete" is a common example of this mistake. Some others are as follows.

|  | Right | Wrong |
|---|---|---|
| disastrous | dih-ZAS-trus | dis-ZASTER-us |
| entrance | ENT-rance | ENTER-ance |
| equipment | ee-QUIP-ment | ee-QUIPT-ment |
| grievous | GREE-vus | GREE-vee-us |
| hindrance | HIND-rance | HIND-er-ance |
| laundry | LAWN-dry | LAWN-der-ry |
| mischievous | MIS-chih-vus | MIS-chee-vi-us |

|  | **Right** | **Wrong** |
|---|---|---|
| modern | MOD-ern | MOD-er-an |
| monstrous | MONS-trus | MONS-ter-us |
| remembrance | re-MEM-brance | re-MEMBER-ance |
| umbrella | um-BRELL-la | um-BEREL-la |

## 1:5c Substitute Sounds

Many words are mispronounced because the speaker substitutes the wrong sound for the correct one. For example, someone might say "ab-SORB-shun" instead of "ab-SORP-shun" for the word **absorption**, which is spelled with a **p**, not a **b**. The following are frequently mispronounced in this way.

|  | **Right** | **Wrong** |
|---|---|---|
| architect | AHR-kih-tekt | AHR-chi-tekt |
| category | CAT-eh-gory | CAT-ah-gory |
| chiropodist | kih-RAHP-uh-dist | chi-RAHP-uh-dist |
| congratulate | con-GRAT-u-late | con-GRAD-u-late |
| diphthong | DIF-thong | DIP-thong |
| frustrated | FRUS-tray-ted | FLUS-tray-ted |
| percolate | PER-kuh-layt | PER-kyoo-layt |
| radiator | RAY-di-ay-ter | RAD-i-ay-ter |
| ribald | RIB-l'd | RYE-bawld |
| similar | SIM-ih-lar | SIM-u-lar |
| strategy | STRAT-eh-ji | STRAD-eh-ji |

## 1:5d Transposed Sounds

Inversion is the reversing of the sequence of two letters in a word. One such inversion always gets a laugh on television. When someone like Archie Bunker says "PRE-vert" instead of "PER-vert" for the word **pervert**, it makes the rest of us feel superior, because we know better. We may unconsciously be making similar mistakes ourselves without realizing it. Here are a few.

|  | **Right** | **Wrong** |
|---|---|---|
| ask | ASK | AKS |
| bronchial | BRONK-ee-al | BRONIK-al |
| larynx | LARR-inx | LAR-nix |
| modern | MOD-ern | MOD-ren |

| | Right | Wrong |
|---|---|---|
| prefer | pre-FER | per-FER |
| perform | per-FORM | pre-FORM |
| perspiration | pers-pir-A-shun | pres-pir-A-shun |

## 1:5e The Silent Letters

Letters which are not pronounced are called **aphthongs**. Most of us don't say "AN-ti-kyoo" for **antique**, except in jest. We know it is pronounced "an-TEEK," but some of the other examples may be less obvious.

| | Right | Wrong |
|---|---|---|
| apropos | ap-ruh-POE | ap-ruh-POZE |
| asthma | AZ-muh | AZTH-muh |
| boatswain | BO-sun | BOAT-swain |
| bouillon | BOO-yun | BULL-yun |
| butte | BYOOT | BUHT-ee |
| comptroller | kun-TRO-lur | comp-TRO-lur |
| corps | KAWR | KAWRPS |
| debris | day-BREE | day-BRISS |
| forehead | FAHR-id | FAWR-hed |
| forte | FORT | for-TAY (except in reference to music) |
| gnome | NOHM | guh-NOH-mee |
| indict | in-DITE | in-DIKT |
| jamb | JAM | JAMB |
| kiln | KILL | KILN |
| palm | PAHM | PAHL'm |
| phlegm | FLEM | FLEG'm |
| proboscis | pro-BAHS-is | pro-BAHS-kiss |
| viscount | VYE-count | VISS-count |

## 1:5f Misplaced Accents

Accenting the wrong syllable is one of the most common pronunciation mistakes. As you know, words ending in **able** are usually accented on the first syllable. There is no other rule to follow in pronouncing words of more than one syllable. It is a matter of remembering the correct accent through frequent use.

The following words are accented on the first syllable.

|  | **Right** | **Wrong** |
|---|---|---|
| alias | AY-lee-us | uh-LYE-us |
| backgammon | BAK-gam'n | bak-GAM'n |
| Broadway | BRAWD-way | brawd-WAY |
| exquisite | EKS-kwi-zit | eks-KWIZ-it |
| finances | FYE-nans-iz | fi-NAN-siz |
| impotent | IM-po-tent | im-PO-tent |
| ignominy | IG-nuh-min-y | ig-nuh-MIN-y |
| impious | IM-pi-uhs | im-PIE-uhs |
| orator | AWR-a-tor | aw-RAY-tor |
| vehement | VEE-he-ment | ve-HEE-ment |

These words are accented on the second syllable.

|  | **Right** | **Wrong** |
|---|---|---|
| acclimate | uh-KLYE-mit | AK-li-mayt |
| adult | uh-DULT | ADD-ult |
| cigar | sih-GAR | SEE-gar |
| clandestine | clan-DES-tin | CLAN-des-tine |
| condolence | kon-DOHL-ens | KAHN-duh-lens |
| defeat | dih-FEET | DEE-feet |
| distributive | dis-TRIB-u-tiv | dis-tri-BEW-tiv |
| exemplary | ex-EM-plary | EX-em-plary |
| inquiry | in-KWIER-y | IN-kwih-ry |
| municipal | myoo-NIS-i-p'l | myoo-ni-SIP'l |
| police | po-LEES | PO-lees |
| remonstrate | reh-MAHN-strayt | REM'n-strayt |
| resource | re-SAWRS | REE-sawrs |
| superfluous | soo-PER-floo-us | soop-er-FLOO-us |

**1:5g** The Secret of Simplicity

In their efforts to pronounce words correctly, some people go overboard and acquire affected pronunciations that they imagine are upper class, like saying "to-MAH-to" for "to-MAY-to."

|  | **Normal** | **Affected** |
|---|---|---|
| after | AFF-ter | AHF-ter |
| aunt | ANT | AHNT |
| beautiful | BYOO-tih-full | BYOO-tee-full |
| dramatist | DRAMM-a-tist | DRAHM-a-tist |
| editor | ED-ih-tur | ED-ih-tawr |

|  | Normal | Affected |
|---|---|---|
| either | EE-ther | EYE-ther |
| fortune | FAWR-chin | FAWR-tyoon |
| illustrate | ILL-us-trate | ih-LUS-trate |
| isolate | EYE-so-late | ISS-uh-late |
| lute | LOOT | LYOOT |
| menu | MEN-yoo | MAY-noo |
| negotiate | ne-GO-shee-ate | ne-GO-see-ate |
| profile | PRO-file | PRO-feel |
| process | PROSS-es | PRO-ses |
| sacrifice | SAK-ra-fice | SAK-ra-fiss |
| secretary | SEK-ra-terry | SEK-ra-tree |
| simultaneous | sy-mul-TAY-neus | sim-mul-TAY-neus |
| stew | STOO | STYOO |
| vase | VAZE | VAHZ |
| vitamin | VY-ta-min | VIT-a-min |

## 1:6 WORDS WITH A FOREIGN ACCENT

Many words used in English speech are of foreign origin, usually Greek, Latin, or French. When **ch** has a hard sound, the word is of Greek or Latin derivation. When **age** has a soft sound, the word comes from the French.

### 1:6a Words Containing CH

|  | Right | Wrong |
|---|---|---|
| Achilles | a-KILL-eez | a-CHILL-eez |
| archives | AHR-kives | AHR-chives |
| chameleon | ka-MEE-lee-on | cha-MEE-lee-on |
| chaos | KAY-os | CHAY-os |
| chasm | KAS'm | CHAS'm |
| Chianti | kee-AHN-tee | chee-AHN-tee |
| chiropodist | kih-ROPP-o-dist | cher-ROPP-o-dist |
| choreography | ko-ree-OG-raff-y | cho-ree-OG-raff-y |
| machinations | mak-a-NAY-shanz | mash-a-NAY-shanz |
| maraschino | mar-as-KEE-no | mar-as-SHE-no |
| zucchini | zoo-KEE-nee | zoo-CHEE-nee |

**1:6b** Words Containing AGE, EGE, or IGE

Words of French derivation ending in **age, ege,** or **ige** have a soft sound. **Corsage** is pronounced "kawr-SAHZH," not "kawr-SAHDJ."

|          | **Right**     | **Wrong**     |
|----------|---------------|---------------|
| barrage  | ba-RAHZH      | ba-RAHDJ      |
| camouflage | KAM-eh-flahzh | KAM-eh-flahdj |
| cortege  | cor-TEHZH     | cor-TEHDJ     |
| garage   | ga-RAHZH      | ga-RAHDJ      |
| massage  | ma-SAHZH      | ma-SAHDJ      |
| menage   | meh-NAHZH     | meh-NAHDJ     |
| prestige | pres-TEEZH    | pres-TEEDJ    |
| sabotage | SAB-a-tahzh   | SAB-a-tahdj   |

## CONCLUSION

The road to correct pronunciation leads to your dictionary. Consult it whenever you're in doubt.

# 2. VOCABULARY ENLARGEMENT

The English language contains about 500,000 words. In addition, there are at least 300,000 technical terms connected with various businesses and professions. You cannot expect to learn all of these, and there is no reason why you should. Twenty to thirty thousand words are quite adequate for the average high school or college graduate. These comprise the words you use yourself or recognize when others use them.

## 2:1 HOW TO RATE YOUR VOCABULARY

You cannot compute the exact size of your own vocabulary, but you can get a general picture of its extent by rating yourself on the following tests. Counting one point for each word you know, 18 is an average score, 25 is a very good score, and 35 is a superior score. (The answers are at the end of the chapter.)

### 2:1a Multiple Choice

Describe the function of each person listed below:

1. An apothecary
   a. utters wise sayings
   b. mixes drugs
   c. abandons his faith

2. A chauvinist
   a. drives a car
   b. hates women
   c. believes in the superiority of his or her own group

3. A cosmopolite
   a. travels the world
   b. lives in the city
   c. is very sophisticated

4. An entomologist
   a. studies words
   b. studies insects
   c. studies human beings

5. A flautist
   a. flouts society
   b. plays the flute
   c. shows off

6. A gaucho
   a. is an acrobatic dancer
   b. herds cattle
   c. is tactless

7. An optician
   a. is an eye doctor
   b. measures visual defects
   c. grinds lenses

8. An orthopedist
   a. specializes in children's diseases
   b. treats foot troubles
   c. treats bone disorders

9. A philatelist
   a. engages in love affairs
   b. donates to charity
   c. collects stamps

10. A raconteur
   a. tells stories well
   b. sings on the stage
   c. is engaged in illegal business

## 2:1b Opposites Attract

Decide which of the following words are similar in meaning and which are opposite:

| | | |
|---|---|---|
| 1. acute | sharp | obtuse |
| 2. brave | cowardly | courageous |

| 3. candor | frankness | hypocrisy |
| 4. effect | cause | consequence |
| 5. fictitious | true | false |
| 6. incarcerate | imprison | liberate |
| 7. judicious | irresponsible | sagacious |
| 8. lustrous | glossy | opaque |
| 9. nefarious | virtuous | wicked |
| 10. taciturn | garrulous | reticent |
| 11. timorous | intrepid | craven |
| 12. verbose | wordy | speechless |

## 2:1c The Match Game

Match the words in column A with the correct meanings in column B.

| **A** | **B** |
| --- | --- |
| 1. ascetic | a. about to occur |
| 2. cajole | b. hidden |
| 3. ecstatic | c. coax |
| 4. feign | d. stiff |
| 5. fluster | e. pretend |
| 6. gaudy | f. disloyalty |
| 7. imminent | g. restore to useful life |
| 8. latent | h. confuse |
| 9. perfidy | i. flashy |
| 10. prosthesis | j. cleanse |
| 11. purge | k. severely abstinent |
| 12. rehabilitate | l. extremely enthusiastic |
| 13. rigid | m. artificial replacement device |
| 14. synthetic | n. substitute for the real thing |

## 2:2 ADD A WORD A WEEK

Learning new words indiscriminately accomplishes little. The words you add should be words that add variety to your usual conversation, words suited to your own particular needs. When, in the course of your reading, television listening, or casual conversation, you come across a word you believe you could use appropriately, make a note of that word. Keep a pencil and paper handy when you sit down to read or watch television, so that you can write down any new word for later reference.

### 2:2a Look It Up

As soon as you have the opportunity, look up the word in the dictionary for exact spelling, meaning, and pronunciation. Do not attempt to use the word until you are absolutely sure of what it means and how it should be pronounced.

After seeing the words in print, you could very well refer to a Freudian slip as "FROO-de-an" instead of "FROY-de-an," or describe a singer as a "PRY-ma-donna" instead of a "PREE-ma-donna." If you decided to use the word **prone**, after hearing someone say, "The injured man was in a prone position when the ambulance arrived," you might assume that **prone** meant lying on one's back, when it actually means lying face down. (**Supine** is the word for lying face upward.)

### 2:2b Write It Down

We have all had the experience of looking up the same word over and over again each time we see it or hear it. We cannot remember the meaning because we have not written it down to imprint it on our memory. Any word you particularly want to remember should be written down on a three by five card, with correct spelling and pronunciation indicated, along with a brief summary of its meaning. Carry the card in your handbag or keep it in a desk drawer where you can refer to it frequently and memorize it perfectly, before attempting to use it. For example:

| | |
|---|---|
| **Spelling** | en er vate |
| **Pronunciation** | ENN-er-vayte |
| **Meaning** | exhaust or weaken |

### 2:2c Put It to Work

Some words would not fit in with your daily conversation but you want to understand them. These words, like **androgyny**, **eponymous**, or **paradigm**, are part of what is known as your recognition vocabulary, which won't be put to frequent use. Any word that is to become part of your spoken vocabulary must be used often in order to remain there. If you want to learn a word a week, you must put those words to work. One of the easiest ways to pick up new words that fit into your usual conversation is to vary your usual speech with synonyms for words you already use.

## 2:3 80 PAIRS OF SYNONYMS AND HOW TO USE THEM

Synonyms do not necessarily have exactly the same meaning. It is these variations that make your speech more interesting. For instance, when you ask, "Do you want to **add** to that statement?" it means, "Have you any additions?" If you ask, "Do you want to **amplify** that statement?" it means, "Do you want to give it a fuller treatment?"

Here are some synonyms, listed in pairs, with definitions.

| | |
|---|---|
| adequate | equal to some requirement |
| satisfactory | satisfying those for whom it is done |
| | |
| adjacent | near one another |
| adjoining | meeting at a boundary line |
| | |
| amazement | an overwhelming condition affecting the intellect |
| astonishment | a similar condition affecting the emotions |
| | |
| beautiful | having harmony and unity |
| lovely | appealing to the senses |
| | |
| behavior | action in the presence of others |
| deportment | behavior as related to a set of rules |
| | |
| bright | shining with original or reflected light |
| brilliant | unusually bright |
| | |
| business | a trade or profession |
| occupation | anything that occupies your time |
| | |
| cancel | to cross out |
| eradicate | to remove all traces |

| | |
|---|---|
| center | an exact point |
| middle | a general area |
| | |
| continual | repeatedly renewed |
| incessant | without end (usually something annoying) |
| | |
| danger | exposure to possible evil |
| peril | exposure to imminent evil |
| | |
| delicious | gratifying to the senses |
| luscious | having an excess of sweetness or richness |
| | |
| difficult | involving skill |
| arduous | involving sustained exertion |
| | |
| equivocal | capable of different interpretations |
| ambiguous | having two possible meanings |
| | |
| example | a sample, specimen, or model |
| archetype | the original model |
| | |
| execute | follow through to the end |
| administer | conduct or carry out |
| | |
| fallacy | a piece of misleading reasoning |
| sophistry | the use of fallacies in reasoning |
| | |
| fear | emotion aroused by threatening evil |
| apprehension | fear of the future |
| | |
| fluctuate | alternate between rise and fall |
| vacillate | hesitate between decisions or actions |
| | |
| general | pertaining equally to all of a class |
| generic | a term referring to every member of a category |
| | |
| generous | giving freely |
| munificent | vast in amount |

| | |
|---|---|
| grief | acute suffering from loss or misfortune |
| anguish | painful, exaggerated grief |
| | |
| happy | enjoying happiness |
| jovial | having a tendency toward merriment |
| | |
| hatred | intense aversion |
| malevolence | having the desire to harm others |
| | |
| healthy | possessing health |
| salubrious | conferring health, as in air or climate |
| | |
| hide | to put out of sight |
| secrete | to hide something in an out-of-the-way place |
| | |
| idle | having no useful occupation |
| indolent | having an aversion to exertion |
| | |
| important | significant |
| momentous | of extreme importance |
| | |
| inherent | naturally existing in something |
| congenital | inborn (usually related to defects) |
| | |
| jealous | fearful of losing something belonging to you |
| envious | begrudging another's success, possessions, etc. |
| | |
| judge | anyone with a capacity for judging |
| referee | chief official in charge of scoring at a game |
| | |
| knowledge | everything the mind knows |
| erudition | deep and extensive learning |
| | |
| large | of more than ordinary size |
| gigantic | exceedingly large |

| | |
|---|---|
| latent | hidden from ordinary observation |
| quiescent | motionless, in a state of inaction |
| | |
| likely | very probable |
| credible | worthy of belief |
| | |
| look | make a conscious endeavor to see |
| behold | fix the sight on something that is clearly seen |
| | |
| make | to cause to exist |
| fabricate | to make a whole out of many parts |
| | |
| melody | simple harmonic composition |
| tune | the entire melody |
| | |
| miscellaneous | chance collection of objects |
| motley | having components of great variety |
| | |
| miserly | seeking to gain by petty savings |
| avaricious | having an eager craving for money |
| | |
| mix | put together indiscriminately |
| blend | make a harmonious mixture |
| | |
| morose | bitterly dissatisfied |
| acrimonious | bitter |
| | |
| mysterious | arousing wonder or curiosity |
| inscrutable | revealing no emotion |
| | |
| name | word by which a person or thing is known |
| apellation | name acquired by a person for some reason |
| | |
| native | belonging by birth (native country) |
| indigenous | native to a country or location (like a plant) |
| | |
| necessary | cannot be otherwise |
| requisite | required |

| | |
|---|---|
| neglect | failure to take reasonable care |
| negligence | habit of neglecting what should be done |
| obscure | not easily discernible |
| abstruse | remote or hidden |
| obsolete | gone out of use |
| obsolescent | going out of use |
| obstinate | refusing to change |
| perverse | acting counter to what is customary |
| old | having existed for a long time |
| elderly | past middle life |
| pay | monetary equivalent for a thing or service |
| emolument | reward for one's work |
| perceive | to see |
| comprehend | to understand completely |
| permanent | not liable to change |
| stable | firmly established |
| persist | adhere to a course, opinion, etc. |
| persevere | persist in the face of obstacles |
| pity | feeling of grief for the misfortunes of others |
| compassion | pity plus sympathy |
| poverty | lack of possessions and luxuries |
| indigence | lack of material comforts |
| quarrel | a dispute in word or action |
| fracas | a disorderly fight |
| question | an interrogation calling for an answer |
| inquiry | a sentence that seeks information |
| quote | to present another's words |
| excerpt | to select a passage from a book or speech |

| | |
|---|---|
| rare | seldom found |
| unique | one of a kind |
| recover | to obtain again after loss |
| retrieve | to recover by effort |
| reliable | having qualities on which you can rely |
| dependable | reliable when the need arises |
| sad | sorrowful or causing sorrow |
| dejected | discouraged |
| secure | free from danger or fear |
| safe | no longer needing to fear or be in danger |
| similarity | said of things or persons somewhat alike |
| resemblance | superficial similarity |
| taciturn | having a disinclination to speak |
| reticent | reluctant to speak out at a given time |
| transaction | something completed |
| proceeding | something in progress |
| transient | not lasting |
| transitory | something that cannot last |
| unite | to form a larger or stronger unit |
| combine | to put together |
| usual | regularly occurring |
| habitual | established practice |
| utility | quality of being useful |
| usefulness | producing results |
| verbal | pertaining to words |
| vocal | pertaining to the voice |
| vigilant | on the lookout against danger |
| cautious | guarding against possibilities of danger or harm |

| violent | involving great force or feeling |
| furious | very violent |

| wealth | accumulation of material things |
| affluence | a state of abundance |

| wisdom | mental power |
| learning | acquired knowledge |

| wit | quick perception of the incongruous |
| humor | the quality of being funny or laughable |

| work | general term for purposeful application of energy |
| labor | physical or mental exertion |

| youthful | possessing youth or young characteristics |
| juvenile | mentally or physically immature |

## 2:4 TIPS ON SAYING WHAT YOU MEAN

We are all guilty of using ambiguous language, especially spoken language, which we have no chance to study and correct. We often say "biannual" (twice a year) when we mean "biennial" (once in two years), or we say "bimonthly" (once in two months) instead of "semimonthly" (twice a month).

Another common ambiguity is the misuse of pronouns, as in the following sentence:

- May talked to Ruth about the way **she** planned to improve the filing system.

The listener does not know who is going to improve the filing system, May or Ruth. In such cases, you must repeat the name of the person to whom you refer.

- May talked to Ruth about the way May planned to improve the filing system.

### 2:4a Correct Word Usage

Still another ambiguity arises from carelessness in word usage, as illustrated in the following instances:

| | |
|---|---|
| alternative | An **alternative** is one of two possibilities. If there are more than two, it is preferable to refer to three, four, or more **choices**. |
| among | **Among** refers to more than two persons or things, as in "**among** the three of us," not "**between** the three of us." |
| amount | **Amount** refers to a certain quantity, while **number** refers to things that can be counted: "There was a large amount of money," or "There were a large number of bills." |
| balance | When speaking of money, you say, "The **balance** is due." Otherwise say, "the **remainder** of the shipment," rather than "the **balance** of the shipment." |
| between | **Between** refers to two people: "**between** you and me." |
| biweekly | This means every two weeks. Use **semiweekly** for twice a week. |
| bring | **Bring** indicates movement toward the speaker: "**Bring** the invoice to me." Otherwise, use **take**: "**Take** this report to the supervisor." |
| criterion | **Criterion** is a test by which something is measured. **Criteria** is the plural and should never be used in place of the singular. |
| data<br>datum | **Data** is the plural form and should not be treated as a singular word: "Here **are** the **data**," not "Here **is** the **data**." |
| done | Do not use instead of **finish**: "The job will be **finished** next week," not "The job will be **done** next week." |
| everybody | **Everybody** is singular and takes a singular pronoun: "**Everybody** brought **his** or **her** (not their) notes to the meeting." |

| | |
|---|---|
| former<br>first | **Former** refers to the first of two things. **First** refers to the first of more than two: "Mr. Jones's **former** wife," "Henry the Eighth's **first** wife." |
| graduate | A person **graduates from** a school or is **graduated from** a school. Never say, "She **graduated** high school." |
| hanged | A person is **hanged**. A mirror is **hung**. |
| individual | This means a particular human being. **Person** is preferable when the meaning is general. |
| join together | Just use **join**, except in a marriage ceremony. |
| kind | Refer to "**that kind**" or "**those kinds**," never "**those kind**." |
| learn | The child **learns**. The instructor **teaches**. |
| less | This means not so much: "There is **less** work to be done than I thought." Say **fewer** when referring to something that can be counted: "She made **fewer** mistakes today." |
| loan | **Lend** is preferable when used as a verb: "Please **lend** me your pen." "I am applying for a **loan**." |
| media | This is the plural of **medium**. Newspapers, radio, and television are **media**. Television is a **medium**. |
| none | This is a singular word requiring a singular verb: "**None** of us **is** going." |
| of | Do not use as a substitute for **have**. Don't say, "I could **of** come in earlier." Say, "I could **have** come in earlier." |
| party | This should refer to more than one person, except in telephone or legal usage. |

| | |
|---|---|
| phenomena | This is the plural of **phenomenon**. Do not use it in a singular sense. Say, "one such **phenomenon**," or "several **phenomena**." |
| regard<br>regards | **Regards** means good wishes and should not be used in place of **regard**, which means reference: "In **regard** to the matter we discussed." |
| rob | A person is **robbed**. A possession is **stolen**. |
| temperature | Degree of warmth or coldness. You **take** your **temperature**. You don't **have** a **temperature**. If your temperature is high, you have a **fever**. |
| virus | You don't **have** a **virus**. You have the result of the virus, a **cold** or the **flu**. |

## 2:5 CHECKING YOUR BUSINESS VOCABULARY

Certain words that are rarely used in ordinary conversation are commonplace in business. Some apply only to special kinds of business, like **codicil** (law), **prognosis** (medicine), or **galley** (publishing). Others are common to most businesses, like **follow-up**, **tickler**, **collating**, **data processing**, and **word processing.**

### 2:5a General Business Vocabulary

Here are a few words relating to the conduct of business:

| | |
|---|---|
| **accrual** | increase by natural growth |
| **adjournment** | postponement of a meeting |
| **affidavit** | statement that is written, signed, and sworn to |
| **agenda** | digest of matters to be treated at a meeting |
| **amortization** | gradual, periodic payment of a debt |
| **automation** | electronic equipment |
| **blueprint** | cheap duplicating method |

| | |
|---|---|
| **bylaws** | rules adopted by a corporation to regulate its conduct |
| **capitalization** | total amount of a corporation's securities |
| **collateral** | something of value deposited as a pledge |
| **collating** | checking sets of typed pages for numerical sequence |
| **combing back** | moving forward reminders of matters requiring attention |
| **consignment** | shipment of goods by owner to selling agent |
| **consolidation** | combination of two or more corporations |
| **controller (comptroller)** | chief accounting officer |
| **data processing** | process by which data are received, stored, rearranged, and transmitted |
| **debentures** | bonds issued without security |
| **depreciation** | loss of value |
| **equity** | net worth |
| **escrow** | conditional delivery of something to a third person |
| **fiscal period** | period covered during one cycle of business operations |
| **follow-up system** | method of filing material so that it will be brought to someone's attention at a certain date |
| **incorporated** | organized into a corporate body |
| **indemnification** | reimbursement for litigation expenses |
| **indexing** | arranging files in alphabetical or numerical order |

| | |
|---|---|
| injunction | a writ by a court of equity, commanding someone to do something or restraining them from doing something |
| insolvent | without the funds to pay debts |
| interface | relationship |
| inventory | all the goods awaiting sale |
| liabilities | debts or obligations of a business |
| lien | a charge making property a security for an obligation |
| liquidation | distribution of assets of a dissolved corporation to stockholders |
| markdown | a reduction below original retail price |
| markup | difference between cost price and selling price |
| minutes | official record of proceedings at a meeting |
| motion | formal proposal for the consideration of those present at a meeting |
| multilithing | reproduction on a small, offset printing press |
| negotiable | capable of being legally transferred from one person to another |
| notarize | to acknowledge or attest a document, as done by a notary public |
| novation | substitution of a new contract for an existing one |
| offset | printing through a photographic process |
| option | an agreement to hold an offer open for a certain period |
| personnel | the body of persons employed by a business |
| photocopy | duplication by Xerox, Thermofax, or similar methods |

| | |
|---|---|
| photostat | reproduction by the same principle as photography |
| portfolio | list of securities owned by an individual or a company |
| posting | transferring debit and credit entries to proper accounts in a ledger |
| proxy | person with authority to vote for absent stockholder |
| quorum | number of persons who must be legally present at a meeting |
| ratio | the relation of one quantity or value to another |
| routing | preparing the mail to go to the persons by whom it should be read |
| screening | procedure to protect executives from handling unimportant phone calls |
| subpoena | an order commanding a person to appear in a legal proceeding |
| tickler | a reminder system |
| word processing | process by which words are received, stored, rearranged, and transmitted |
| yield | annual percentage rate of return on an investment |

## 2:6 WORD ROOTS AS A GUIDE TO WORD MEANINGS

A person familiar with the Greek or Latin origins of English words can usually guess an unfamiliar word's meaning. This is not to suggest that you should study Greek and Latin, but you will be able to understand words better when you recognize their origins. For instance, **bi** and **tri** are the Latin roots meaning **two** and **three**. Because of this, you know immediately that a bicycle is a two-wheeler and a tricycle is a three-wheeler. You know that a centennial is a one-hundredth anniversary, from the Latin **cent** meaning **hundred**, so a bicentennial is obviously a two-hundredth anniversary.

## 2:6a Some Sample Roots

| Root | Meaning | Example | Meaning |
|------|---------|---------|---------|
| abol (L. **abolere**) | do away with | abolish | do away with |
| acm (G. **acme**) | top | acme | top |
| acu (L. **acurere**) | sharpen | acumen | sharpness |
| aesth (G. **aisthomai**) | feel | anaesthetic | something that destroys feeling |
| ag (L. **agere**) | drive | coagulate | drive together |
| agog (G. **agogos**) | leader | demagogue | false leader |
| agr (L. **agr**) | land | agrarian | relating to land |
| alb (L. **albus**) | white | albumen | white of an egg |
| alt (L. **altus**) | high | altitude | height |
| ambul (L. **ambulare**) | walk | somnambulist | sleepwalker |
| ampl (L. **amplu**) | large | amplify | enlarge upon |
| anim (L. **animus**) | soul | magnanimous | great-souled |
| apert (L. **apertus**) | open | aperture | opening |
| aqu (L. **aqua**) | water | aquatic | living in water |
| aug (L. **augere**) | increase | augment | increase |
| bell (L. **bellum**) | war | belligerent | aggressive |
| bene (L. **bene**) | well | benevolent | well-wishing |
| bibl (L. **biblos**) | book | bibliography | list of books |
| calor (L. **calor**) | heat | calorie | unit of heat and energy |
| carn (L. **carnis**) | flesh | carnal | fleshly |
| cede (L. **cedere**) | go | antecedent | going before |
| celer (L. **celer**) | swift | accelerate | go faster |
| cent (L. **centum**) | hundred | centennial | occurring every hundred years |
| cern (L. **cernere**) | separate | discern | distinguish |
| chrom (G. **chrome**) | color | chromatic | relating to color |
| cinct (L. **cinctus**) | bind | succinct | compressed |
| cognit (L. **cognitus**) | know | incognito | unknown |
| culp (L. **culpa**) | blame | culpable | blamable |
| curs (L. **cursus**) | run | cursory | running along |
| decim (L. **decimus**) | ten | decimal | number using base of 10 |
| doct (L. **doctus**) | teach | doctrine | something taught |
| empt (L. **emptus**) | take | exempt | take out |

| Root | Meaning | Example | Meaning |
|------|---------|---------|---------|
| etymo (G. **etymos**) | true | etymology | true sources of words |
| fa (L. **fari**) | speak | affable | easily spoken to |
| fac (L. **facere**) | make | facsimile | made alike |

You cannot expect to learn all of the word roots, nor do you need to do so. It is just a way of reminding yourself where words come from, taking the mystery out of it.

## 2:6b Derivations of Business Words

The derivations of some business terms are an interesting story in themselves. According to Wilfred Funk, the language authority, the word **bank** came from the old Italian word **banca,** meaning "bench." The early bankers, or money-changers, did their business on a bench. As for **bankrupt**, the **rupt** part of the word means "broken" in Latin, so the man who is bankrupt has a broken bench.

The word **boss** comes from the Dutch Colonial days in New York City, when a master workman was called by the Dutch word **baas**, and it soon became part of the American language.

In Rome, 2000 years ago, a merchant figured his profits and losses by using **calculi** or "little stones" as counters, from which we derive our words **calculate** and **calculator**.

A **stenographer** is someone who takes dictation in shorthand, from the Greek words for "compact" and "write," **steno** and **grapho**. A **secretary** is one who keeps a business-person's confidences, from the Latin term **secretarius**, meaning "one who keeps your secrets."

The **salary** the secretary receives is from the Latin **salarium**, or "salt allowance." Salt was considered a necessary part of the diet, so part of a Roman soldier's wages was for the purpose of buying salt.

## ANSWERS TO TESTS

### Multiple Choice

| | |
|---|---|
| 1. b | 6. b |
| 2. c | 7. c |
| 3. a | 8. c |
| 4. b | 9. c |
| 5. b | 10. a |

### Opposites Attract

| | similar | opposite |
|---|---|---|
| 1. acute | sharp | obtuse |
| 2. brave | courageous | cowardly |
| 3. candor | frankness | hypocrisy |
| 4. effect | consequence | cause |
| 5. fictitious | false | true |
| 6. incarcerate | imprison | liberate |
| 7. judicious | sagacious | irresponsible |
| 8. lustrous | glossy | opaque |
| 9. nefarious | wicked | virtuous |
| 10. taciturn | reticent | garrulous |
| 11. timorous | craven | intrepid |
| 12. verbose | wordy | speechless |

### The Match Game

| | |
|---|---|
| 1. k | 8. b |
| 2. c | 9. f |
| 3. l | 10. m |
| 4. e | 11. j |
| 5. h | 12. g |
| 6. i | 13. d |
| 7. a | 14. n |

## CONCLUSION

There is only one sure way to gain a larger vocabulary: Learn words you can use, and put them to work.

# 3. WORDS AND EXPRESSIONS TO AVOID

## 3:1 CLICHÉS

Clichés are so much a part of our vocabulary that we use them automatically. Take note of the clichés you use during the course of one day, and you will be surprised at their number. You do not need to eliminate them entirely from your speech. Just watch out for the ones you use too frequently. Everyone has his or her favorites that he or she repeats almost unconsciously. Sometimes there is no other way to say exactly what you mean in the most concise way. For instance, "This car is a **lemon**." Used occasionally and appropriately, clichés can emphasize a point, but you should try to use them with discretion.

### 3:1a 50 Clichés to Screen Out

Every cliché, when it originated, was a colorful description of something. Constant use, however, has caused such expressions to lose their original flavor. Most of the following could be dropped without much loss:

1. acid test
2. almighty dollar
3. avoid like the plague
4. better late than never
5. bitter end
6. bundle of nerves
7. clear as a bell
8. cold as ice
9. cool as a cucumber
10. dirty old man
11. doting parent
12. easy mark

13. filthy lucre
14. flat as a pancake
15. fly off the handle
16. get the sack
17. give the gate
18. go to pieces
19. has a screw loose
20. head over heels
21. holding the bag
22. in the same boat
23. irons in the fire
24. join the club
25. know the ropes
26. let your hair down
27. limp as a rag
28. live it up
29. make ends meet
30. method in her madness
31. misery loves company

32. never a dull moment
33. no place like home
34. no strings attached
35. old as the hills
36. on cloud nine
37. over a barrel
38. pale as a ghost
39. perish the thought
40. put the bite on
41. red as a beet
42. ring a bell
43. ripe old age
44. sell like hot cakes
45. shake a leg
46. shoot the breeze
47. thin as a rail
48. turn up your nose
49. under the wire
50. with bated breath

**3:2** 45 EXAMPLES OF BUSINESS JARGON

Businesspeople have their own clichés, like **update** or **finalize**. Like other clichés, these have their uses, until they become dated and trite. Try to think of some alternative expressions if you find yourself using any of the following too frequently:

1. advance planning
2. all things being equal
3. at this point in time
4. auspicious occasion
5. back to the drawing board
6. carry a lot of weight
7. carry the ball
8. cash in on
9. cash on the barrel
10. concept
11. consensus of opinion
12. contact (as a verb)
13. co-opt

14. ear to the ground
15. expertise
16. field of endeavor
17. finalize
18. foreseeable future
19. frame of reference
20. get a line on
21. get the sack
22. in short supply
23. in the final analysis
24. kick an idea around
25. know the ropes
26. lick into shape
27. moot point

28. no strings attached
29. off the record
30. ongoing
31. operative
32. -oriented (as part of a compound word)
33. pass the buck
34. play it by ear
35. set up shop
36. smart money
37. spread yourself thin
38. stonewall
39. subsume
40. swing a deal
41. think tank
42. update
43. viable alternative
44. whole ball of wax
45. -wise (used as a suffix)

## 3:3 TIRESOME VOGUE EXPRESSIONS

In any period there are words and expressions that turn up in everyone's vocabulary. At first, using them seems like an "in" thing to do, but after a time they become habitual and rather tiresome usages. Here are five that come to mind:

hopefully
I couldn't care less
have a good day
meaningful relationship
beautiful person

These have been used so much that people say them mechanically, with little regard for their meaning.

### 3:3a "Hopefully"

**Hopefully** originally meant "with hope" or "in a hopeful manner." Its current usage, to mean "it is to be hoped" or "let us hope," is not accepted by strict grammarians. It would not only be less trite to avoid using **hopefully** this way, but it would also be more grammatically correct. Say instead, "I hope" or "We hope" that a certain event will transpire, rather than "Hopefully, the new campaign will be a success," or "Hopefully, I'll get a raise this year."

### 3:3b "I Couldn't Care Less"

**I couldn't care less**, meaning "I really don't care," is not a bad expression; it is just overused. Try to use it less frequently and, above all, don't corrupt it into "I could care less." The latter corruption is often used by people who don't realize that they are actually saying, "I do care somewhat."

### 3:3c "Have a Good Day"

Have a good day is a pleasant enough greeting, but when everybody says it to everyone else, and on all occasions, it becomes a bit ridiculous. Some people vary it with "Have a good morning" (or afternoon, evening, weekend), which helps, but not much. When one is constantly being told to have a good day, the phrase can go beyond triteness to become downright irritating. It is better to omit this or find a substitute.

### 3:3d "Meaningful"

A person no longer has a serious love affair; he or she has a "meaningful relationship." People also have "meaningful experiences" or "meaningful dialogues." Meaningful conveys a positive feeling toward an experience, a dialogue, or a relationship, but it is rather vague. Be more specific. Have a "serious relationship," an "interesting experience," or a "productive dialogue."

### 3:3e "Beautiful Person"

This is another dated generalization. Say instead, "I like her," "I know you'll like her," or "She's very likeable."

All such words and expressions eventually go out of vogue and, if you get into the habit of using them, you are not only lacking in originality, but you are dating yourself as well.

### 3:4 SLANG AND ITS USE

Can you remember when everyone was either uptight or feeling groovy, and people had hangups or good vibes and bad vibes? Such slang expressions should be eliminated if you don't want to seem out of date. Some of them, like uptight and hangups, are still in use, but it would be evidence of a better vocabulary to substitute more traditional expressions like, "I'm feeling tense,"

"I'm apprehensive," or "She is so conventional." Instead of referring to **hangups**, describe them as **inhibitions** or **fixations**.

## 3:4a Dated Slang

Some slang words are shorter ways of saying things that have been incorporated into the language, like **auto, bus, intercom, cab, taxi, exam, phone, piano,** and **zoo**. No one speaks of an **automobile, omnibus,** or **zoological garden** any more. Other slang expressions like **and how!** and **corny** are still used by some people in spite of their datedness, along with **cool, square, far-out,** and **chintzy**. Avoid frequent use of such expressions when they are new, and be the first to drop them when they have been around awhile. They will soon be as antiquated as **cake-eater, cat's whiskers,** and **twenty-three skidoo**.

## 3:4b Vulgar Slang

You must learn to discriminate in your use of slang and avoid expressions that coarsen your speech. The use of vulgarisms indicates a lack of respect, not only for your listeners, but also for yourself. The so-called "four-letter words," which were once spoken only by men, are being used more frequently by women since the advent of women's liberation. This may be excusable occasionally, when you are among close friends, but it does not add to your stature in public. There are other slang vulgarisms which, though they are not obscene, indicate a lack of refinement, such as:

1. get off my back
2. in the bag
3. on the ball
4. get a bang out of
5. get to first base
6. bawling out
7. beat your brains out
8. a belt
9. big mouth
10. bilge
11. put the bite on
12. a blast
13. booze
14. broad
15. bug off
16. burned up
17. butt out
18. can (toilet)
19. chew the fat
20. clip joint
21. drop dead
22. eightball
23. floozy
24. hogwash

25. jerk
26. kick the bucket
27. loot

28. monkey business
29. nuts!
30. ripped off

31. scram

### 3:4c Slang to Use with Discretion

Slang can add color to your speech if it is used only occasionally, for emphasis or for humor, but not if it peppers your language. Here are a few expressions for saying what you want in the shortest possible way. Use them discreetly.

1. call it quits
2. cheapskate
3. the chips are down
4. dead duck
5. disc jockey
6. double take
7. in drag
8. dropout
9. eager beaver
10. falsie
11. fed up
12. a fix
13. footsie
14. free load
15. gimmick
16. goof-off

17. grouse
18. hard time
19. hassle
20. Ivy League
21. jalopy
22. kicks
23. lay an egg
24. needle
25. oddball
26. picnic
27. red carpet
28. send-off
29. take the cake
30. through the mill
31. under the table
32. visiting fireman

33. wet blanket

### 3:5 BAD HABITS OF SPEECH AND HOW TO OVERCOME THEM

There are two extremes of speech that are equally bad habits. One is the use of fancy words under the impression that fancy is better, when quite the opposite is true. The other is the use of incorrect words because the correct ones sound strange and you are not in the habit of using them.

**3:5a** Simple Language Is Best

Certain words have been so overused that they have lost much of their force and meaning. Many of us have a tendency to use fancy words like **hilarious, fabulous,** and **marvelous,** when we simply mean **funny, astonishing,** and **wonderful.** The use of the word **gross** to cover anything you do not like is another example of this kind of exaggerated speech. Keep it simple, and you will be following the examples of Abraham Lincoln and Ernest Hemingway, who used speech of extreme simplicity and effectiveness.

| Fancy | Simple |
|---|---|
| absolutely | yes |
| acidulous | sour |
| ambiance | atmosphere |
| ameliorate | improve |
| antipathy | aversion |
| bellicose | quarrelsome |
| bizarre | unusual |
| blaspheme | swear |
| bourgeois | middle class |
| bovine | cowlike |
| calumny | false statement |
| capitulate | surrender |
| celerity | speed |
| celibate | unmarried |
| cinema | movie |
| confrontation | meeting |
| debacle | collapse |
| décolleté | low cut |
| defunct | dead |
| delineate | describe |
| ecumenical | universal |
| eleemosynary | charitable |
| embryonic | undeveloped |
| emolument | salary |
| encounter | meet |
| fallacious | false |
| fantastic | great, unusual |

| Fancy | Simple |
|-------|--------|
| fastidious | particular |
| felicitous | appropriate |
| firmament | sky |
| garniture | decoration |
| gourmandize | eat well |
| halitosis | bad breath |
| hirsute | hairy |
| hypertension | high blood pressure |
| idiosyncrasy | peculiarity |
| inimical | hostile |
| invidious | offensive |
| lachrymose | tearful |
| libation | drink |
| lubricious | lecherous |
| masticate | chew |
| mendacious | untruthful |
| moribund | dying |
| nebulous | vague |
| necromancy | sorcery |
| obese | fat |
| osculate | kiss |
| penurious | stingy |
| perspicacious | discerning |
| pharmacy | drugstore |
| posture | attitude |
| precipitous | steep |
| querulous | complaining |
| salubrious | healthful |
| sobriquet | nickname |
| supernumerary | extra |
| underprivileged | poor |

**3:5b** Don't Be Afraid to Speak Correctly

In their zeal to avoid affectation, some speakers deliberately use incorrect words and constructions because they feel that the correct ones sound pretentious. Whether such poor usage is deliberate or accidental, it should be avoided.

| Incorrect | Correct |
| --- | --- |
| aggravate | irritate |
| ahold of | hold of |
| ain't | isn't |
| anyways | anyway |
| anywheres | anywhere |
| aren't I | am I not |
| as to whether | whether |
| barge in | enter |
| being as | since |
| busted | burst |
| can't hardly | can hardly |
| character | person |
| class | style |
| complected | complexioned |
| could of | could have |
| drapes | draperies, curtains |
| drug | dragged |
| enthused | was enthusiastic |
| fed up | disgusted |
| for free | free |
| gal | woman |
| guy | man |
| have got | have |
| heartrendering | heartrending |
| heighth | height |
| I been | I have been |
| I begun | I began |
| I done | I did |
| invite (noun) | invitation |
| irregardless | regardless |
| I seen | I saw |
| kind of | rather |
| leave | let |
| liable | likely |
| loan (verb) | lend |
| love | like |
| mad at | angry with |
| might of | might have |
| most | almost |

| Incorrect | Correct |
|---|---|
| off of | off |
| over with | over |
| party | person |
| providing | provided |
| quote (noun) | quotation |
| refined | genteel |
| reoccur | recur |
| she says | she said |
| snuck | sneaked |
| start off | start |
| supposing | suppose |
| swang | swung |
| that there | that |
| theirselves | themselves |
| them (adjective) | those |
| this here | this |
| try and | try to |
| type | kind |
| umble | humble |
| unawares | unaware |
| unbeknownst | unknown |
| wait on | wait for |
| youse | you |

## 3:6 FRENCH WORDS—THEIR USE AND MISUSE

Standard French expressions like **faux pas** and **tête-à-tête** are understood by nearly everyone, and there is no need to use English equivalents. The more unusual French words like **abattoir, accouchement,** and **atelier** must be used with discretion, since it is impolite to use foreign words that your listener may not know. Never use an unfamiliar French word or phrase to show off your superior knowledge; that is the height of rudeness.

### 3:6a Standard French Words

Many French words have become fully incorporated into the English language.

| | | | |
|---|---|---|---|
| a la carte | chalet | entree | pique |
| a la mode | chamois | faux pas | pompon |
| aperitif | champagne | fiance´ | portiere |
| argot | chapeau | foyer | premiere |
| au gratin | chaperon | garage | prestige |
| au revoir | charlatan | garcon | proté´ge´ |
| ballet | chateau | gourmet | puré´e |
| bandeau | chauffeur | hors d'oeuvre | regime |
| bas-relief | chef | jabot | rendezvous |
| batiste | chemise | julienne | repertoire |
| baton | chic | layette | restaurant |
| beau | chiffon | lingerie | ré´sume´ |
| beige | clairvoyant | lorgnette | revue |
| belle | cliche´ | madame | Roquefort |
| bonbon | cognac | mademoiselle | roue´ |
| bon jour | coiffeur | massage | roulette |
| boudoir | comedienne | masseur | sabotage |
| bouillabaisse | compote | masseuse | sachet |
| bouillon | connoisseur | matinee | sauté´ |
| boulevard | consomme´ | mayonnaise | seance |
| bouquet | corps | menu | silhouette |
| bourgeoise | corsage | meringue | souffle´ |
| bric-a-brac | crepe | migraine | suede |
| brochure | cretonne | modiste | surveillance |
| bureau | croquette | moire´ | tableau |
| cabaret | cuisine | monsieur | table d'hôte |
| cafe´ | debutante | morgue | tête-à-tête |
| Camembert | dé´collete´ | naive | trousseau |
| camisole | eclair | negligee | vaudeville |
| camouflage | elite | pâte´ de foie gras | velour |
| canape´ | en route | personnel | |
| carafe | ensemble | petite | |

**3:6b** French Words to Use with Restraint

When you are talking to sophisticated people, you can use words and phrases like the following. There should be no misunderstanding, but use them sparingly. It sounds affected to sprinkle French too liberally throughout your conversation, and it is better, at times, to use the English equivalent.

| French Word | English Equivalent |
|---|---|
| abattoir | slaughterhouse |
| accouchement | parturition, childbirth |
| amour | love |
| atelier | workshop, studio |
| attaché | diplomatic official |
| au courant | up-to-date |
| au naturel | naked, uncooked |
| banquette | upholstered bench |
| baroque | ornate |
| barrage | concentrated fire |
| beau monde | fashionable society |
| belles-lettres | literature |
| bête noir | someone you fear |
| bijou | jewel |
| bonhomie | good nature |
| bon mot | witticism |
| cache | something hidden |
| camaraderie | goodwill |
| canard | false report, hoax |
| carillon | set of bells |
| carte blanche | unconditional power |
| chef-d'oeuvre | masterpiece |
| chignon | roll, knot, bun (hair) |
| claque | paid applauders |
| cloisonné | enameled decoration |
| communiqué | official report |
| contretemps | embarrassing situation |
| cortege | funeral procession |
| coterie | exclusive group |
| critique | critical review |
| debacle | sudden collapse |
| debris | rubble |
| déclassé | lowered in class |
| déjeuner | breakfast |
| denouement | climax, outcome |
| de rigueur | fashionable, customary |
| dernier cri | latest thing |
| deshabille | undressed |
| distingué | distinguished |

| French Word | English Equivalent |
|---|---|
| dossier | documents on a subject |
| double-entendre | with two meanings |
| élan | spirit, dash |
| embonpoint | obesity, fat |
| en rapport | in agreement |
| entourage | attendants |
| entre´ nous | secretly, confidentially |
| expose´ | exposure |
| fait accompli | accomplished fact |
| gamin | waif |
| gauche | tactless |
| gourmand | glutton |
| grande passion | love affair |
| habitue´ | regular |
| hauteur | haughty manner |
| idée fixe | obsession |
| impasse | deadlock |
| ingénue | innocent girl |
| lese majesty | irreverence |
| liaison | affair |
| macabre | ghastly |
| malaise | discomfort, uneasiness |
| mélange | mixture |
| melee | free-for-all |
| ménage | household |
| nee | born |
| nom de plume | pen name |
| nuance | subtle distinction |
| panache | stylish manner |
| par excellence | epitome |
| parvenu | upstart |
| pas de deux | dance for two |
| pastiche | incongruous mixture |
| patois | dialect, jargon |
| persiflage | banter |
| pièce de résistance | most important item |
| pied-à-terre | part-time residence |
| pince-nez | eyeglasses clipped to the nose |
| poseur | affected person |

| French Word | English Equivalent |
| --- | --- |
| potpourri | medley |
| précis | summary |
| raconteur | story teller |
| raison d'être | reason for being |
| recherche' | choice |
| retrousse' | turned up |
| richochet | rebound |
| risque' | suggestive |
| rococo | elaborately ornamented |
| salon | drawing room |
| savoir-faire | know-how |
| succès d'estime | critical success |

## CONCLUSION

In your choice of language, as in anything else, you are known by the company you keep—so choose carefully.

# 4. SENTENCE STRUCTURE

Spoken English is more informal than its written counterpart, but it must still be grammatically correct. You can end a sentence with a preposition without sounding illiterate, and it is perfectly all right to use contractions like **don't** and **won't**.

If a secretary were to say, "Mr. Axelrod **will not** be in this afternoon, and I **do not** expect him until Wednesday," it might give the impression of extreme formality almost to the point of coldness.

Likewise, "**To whom** do you wish to speak?" sounds affected compared with the more informal, "Whom do you wish to speak **to?**"

## 4:1 NINE WAYS TO SAY THINGS BETTER

Your speech should be casual but not vulgar. Double negatives should be avoided, along with other careless usages. The following is simple advice on the correction of nine typical mistakes.

### 4:1a Avoid Double Negatives

Two negative words in the same statement produce what is known as a double negative. This usage was acceptable in Shakespeare's time, but it is considered poor English today.

Poor:    I **can't** find that memo **nowhere**.
Better:  I **can** find that memo **nowhere**.
           I **can't** find that memo **anywhere**.

| Poor: | I can't hardly read his writing. |
|---|---|
| Better: | I can hardly read his writing. |
| | I can't read his writing. |

## 4:1b Use Correct Past Tense

There are several mistakes you could make with the past tenses of verbs. First, you might use the past participle instead of the past tense. Take the verb **to see** as an example:

| Present Tense: | I **see** the new supervisor over there. |
|---|---|
| Past Tense: | I **saw** the new supervisor yesterday. |
| Past Participle: | I **have seen** the new supervisor every day. |

The confusion of **saw** with **seen** is a common mistake.

| Poor: | I **seen** the new supervisor yesterday. |
|---|---|
| Better: | I **saw** the new supervisor yesterday. |

Another such error adds **ed** to verbs that should form their past tenses by a complete change in spelling.

| Poor: | My dress **shrinked** in the wash. |
|---|---|
| Better: | My dress **shrank** in the wash. |

## 4:1c Modify Verbs with Adverbs

We often confuse adjectives and adverbs in our daily speech. An adjective should modify only a noun or pronoun. Do not use an adjective to modify a verb.

| Poor: | He **dictates** too **rapid**. |
|---|---|
| Better: | He **dictates** too **rapidly**. |

## 4:1d Modify Adjectives with Adverbs

Do not use an adjective to modify another adjective.

| Poor: | This is a **real good** typewriter. |
|---|---|
| Better: | This is a **really good** typewriter. |

## 4:1e Learn the Use of BAD and BADLY

After verbs that express actions of the senses, like **feel, look,** smell, **sound**, and **taste**, you must use the adjective **bad** rather than the adverb **badly**.

> **Poor:** I feel **badly** about that.
> **Better:** I feel **bad** about that.

In other cases the reverse is true, and you may use the adverb as usual.

> **Poor:** They **need** help **bad**.
> **Better:** They **need** help **badly**.

## 4:1f Learn the Use of GOOD and WELL

After verbs that express actions of the senses, like **feel, look, smell, sound,** and **taste**, you must use the adjective **good** rather than the adverb **well.**

> **Poor:** The report **looks well**.
> **Better:** The report **looks good**.

In other cases the reverse is true, and you may use the adverb as usual.

> **Poor:** She **did good** the first day on the job.
> **Better:** She **did well** the first day on the job.

**Exception:** You say "I feel well," when talking about your health, but you said "I feel good," when you mean that you are in a good mood.

## 4:1g Remember the Subjunctive (WAS and WERE)

When you are expressing a wish or a supposition, you use the subjunctive mood. The best example of this is the use of **was** and **were. Was** is in the indicative mood and is used to declare a fact: I **was** there at the time.

**Were** is in the subjunctive mood and is used to speculate: I wish I **were** there when it happened.

Here are some more instances of poor usage that you should guard against when describing conditions contrary to fact or highly improbable:

> **Poor:** If I **was** rich I'd travel around the world.
> **Better:** If I **were** rich I'd travel around the world.

Poor:     She acts as if she **was** the person in charge.

Better:   She acts as if she **were** the person in charge.

### 4:1h Be Careful with I and ME

Everyone knows that the following sentences should read:

● He gave the correspondence **to me.**

**or**

● I handled the correspondence **for him.**

Confusion arises when the sentences are slightly more complicated.

**Poor:**    He dictated the correspondence to **Mary** and I.

**Better:**  He dictated the correspondence to **Mary** and **me**.

**Poor:**    It **was me** who handled the correspondence.

**Better:**  It **was I** who handled the correspondence.

**Rule 1**: Always use **me** after a preposition, no matter what words come between the two.

**Rule 2**: Always use I after the verb **to be**.

### 4:1i Watch Out for WHO and WHOM

**Who** is used as the subject of a verb, while **whom** is used as the object of a verb or preposition. Sometimes the use is obvious:

● He is the official **to whom** I mailed the notice.

● She is the secretary **who works** for Mr. Jones.

The usage becomes confusing when **who** or **whom** is separated from the verb of which it is the subject or object.

● **Whom** would you like to meet? (object)

● **Who** shall I say is calling? (subject)

### 4:2 A GUIDE TO CLARITY OF MEANING

When people don't say what they mean, it can cause all sorts of disasters, from broken appointments to the loss of important accounts. Think before you speak. An omitted or misplaced word or phrase can convey an entirely different meaning from the one you intended.

## 4:2a Sins of Omission

Omission of a word can cause unnecessary confusion.

**Confusing:** The secretary and treasurer resigned.

This sounds as if you are talking about **one** officer of the company, when in reality you mean **two**.

**Clear:** The secretary and **the** treasurer resigned.

Here is another appropriate example:

**Confusing:** Mr. Calhoun likes the word processing system better than his secretary.

This could mean that Mr. Calhoun likes the system better than his secretary does, or that Mr. Calhoun likes the system better than he likes his secretary.

**Clear:** Mr. Calhoun likes the word processing system better than his secretary **does**.

## 4:2b Misplaced Modifiers

Modifiers should be placed immediately before or after the words they modify. If you change their positions, you change the meaning of the sentence.

**Confusing:** I saw the new computer **getting off the elevator**.

**Clear:** **Getting off the elevator**, I saw the new computer.

The bold phrase modifies the word **I**, and should be placed next to it. Otherwise, you give the impression that the computer is getting off the elevator.

You can make the sentence even clearer if you add the conjunction **while**.

**Clearer:** **While** getting off the elevator, I saw the new computer.

### 4:2c Ambiguous Modifiers

When you use a modifier between two words, both of which it could modify, the meaning of the sentence is obscured.

Confusing:    A taxpayer who cheats frequently gets penalized.

Is the speaker talking about a taxpayer who cheats frequently, or one who frequently gets penalized?

Clear:    A taxpayer who **frequently cheats** gets penalized.

**or**

A taxpayer who cheats gets **penalized frequently**.

### 4:2d Ambiguous References

Pronouns like **this, which, they,** or **that** are often used carelessly. Although the person you are talking to usually understands what you mean, the meaning can sometimes be misinterpreted.

Confusing:
1. Our secretaries have all been to college. **This** is a qualification that we require.
2. Miss Dennis is going to Canada. **They** are interested in using our services.
3. I can't give you that information until Mr. Evans gets back, **which** is unfortunate.

Clear:
1. Our secretaries have all been to college. **A college education** is a qualification that we require.
2. Miss Dennis is going to Canada. **The Canadians** are interested in using our services.
3. **Unfortunately,** I can't give you that information until Mr. Evans gets back.

Always use a noun instead of a pronoun if the use of the pronoun could cause confusion.

Confusing:    Mr. Fawcett promoted Mr. Graves after **he** had only worked here for six months.

It is not clear whether **he** refers to Mr. Fawcett or Mr. Graves.

**Clear**: Mr. Fawcett promoted Mr. Graves, after **Mr. Graves** had worked here for only six months.

**or**

After Mr. Graves had worked here for only six months, Mr. Fawcett promoted him.

## 4:3 MAKING THE RIGHT CONNECTIONS

A conjunction connects words and groups of words. **And, but**, and **so** are the most commonly used, but a more precise use of conjunctions can make your meaning clearer. As you can see in the following examples, a simple change of conjunctions gives entirely different meanings:

- I am going to eat lunch **and** go shopping.
- I am going to eat lunch, **then** go shopping.
- I am going to eat lunch **or** go shopping.

The first sentence expresses simple addition by the use of **and**. The second sentence expresses a time lapse by the use of **then**. The third sentence indicates a choice of alternatives by the use of **or**.

Choose your conjunctions carefully and do not limit yourself. Become familiar with the various conjunctions and their use, so that no one can mistake your meaning.

### 4:3a 15 Ways to Use Conjunctions

Suppose you were to tell your boss, "**When** I asked for an appointment for you with Mr. Haven, his secretary was not sure that he could make it."

It would be much more precise to say, "**Although** I asked for an appointment for you with Mr. Haven, his secretary was not sure that he could make it."

**When** simply means **at the time**, but **although** means **in spite of the fact that** and indicates more concern on your part.

The following list is a reminder of the uses of the various conjunctions, so that you can learn to pick those that will help you express yourself most clearly.

1. **Addition**
   To express an added thought or idea, use conjunctions such as **and, again, also, besides, both, finally, further, furthermore, in addition, likewise, moreover, too.**
   **Example:** I have completed the contracts **in addition** to typing the enclosure letters.

2. **Choice**
   To indicate a choice use **else, either or, neither nor, nor, or, otherwise.**
   **Example:** I can **either** get out the correspondence **or** make these important phone calls.

3. **Comparison**
   For making comparisons, use **as, than, as much as, more than.**
   **Example:** I did not accomplish **as much as** I would have liked.

4. **Concession**
   To concede something, use **admitting that, although, assuming that, even if, no matter how, of course, though.**
   **Example:** I would not go, **even if** I had the chance.

5. **Consequence**
   To indicate a consequence, use **accordingly, as a consequence, as a result, consequently, hence, in this way, so, then, therefore, thus.**
   **Example:** Mr. Jones gave me these instructions, **so** I will follow them.

6. **Contrast**
   Show contrast by using conjunctions such as **and yet, but, however, in contrast to, in spite of, nevertheless, nor, notwithstanding, on the contrary, still, unfortunately, whereas, yet.**
   **Example:** She finished her work, **in spite of** the interruptions.

7. **Extent**
   To show extent, use conjunctions such as **as, according, as far as, more than, rather than, so.**
   **Example:** I felt the heat today, **more than** at any other time this summer.

8. **Emphasis**

   If you wish to repeat an idea in order to emphasize it, use **and assuredly, as I have said, certainly, for example, in fact, in other words, undoubtedly.**

   **Example:** This has been a red letter day; **in fact,** everything has gone unusually well.

9. **Explanation**

   When you wish to explain something, use **because, for, for example, for instance, in particular, more specifically, specifically.**

   **Example:** We should devise some new systems; **for instance,** a more efficient way of routing the mail.

10. **Location**

    There are two words to indicate location: **where** and **wherever.**

    **Example:** Our salespeople travel **wherever** their territory requires it.

11. **Purpose**

    Conjunctions to indicate purpose are **in order that, lest, that, why.**

    **Example:** That is the reason **why** the salesperson is going to Rochester.

12. **Reason**

    Conjunctions that indicate reason are **as, because, for, since, whereas.**

    **Example:** The salesperson is going to Rochester **since** that is part of his territory.

13. **Supposition**

    Supposition or condition is indicated by **except, if, otherwise, provided, supposing, unless.**

    **Example:** I'll leave early, **provided** I can get the time off.

14. **Result**

    A result is indicated by the use of **because, of which, but that, on account of which, so that, that is.**

    **Example:** I have arranged my schedule **so that** I can lunch at one o'clock.

15. **Time**

    Time is indicated by using **after, as, as long as, before,** meanwhile, now that, since, until, when, whenever, while.

**Example:** The workload will slacken **after** the holidays are over.

## 4:4 KEYS TO CORRECT SENTENCE STRUCTURE

It has been said that the simple, declarative sentence is one of the greatest inventions of human intelligence. A sentence that is clear, correct, and effective performs an important function in communication. You cannot stop to consider grammatical correctness every time you open your mouth to speak, but you can watch out for flaws and try to avoid the most glaring ones in your own speech.

### 4:4a Unnecessary ANDS and BUTS

A common error in sentence structure is the insertion of **and** or **but** before the words **which** or **who**.

**Wrong:**   She is an intelligent woman, **and who** is an industrious worker.

This is a beautiful typewriter, **and which** you will enjoy using.

He showed much enthusiasm at first, **but which** soon evaporated.

**Right:**   She is an intelligent woman, **who** is an industrious worker.

This is a beautiful typewriter, **which** you will enjoy using.

He showed much enthusiasm at first, **which** soon evaporated.

### 4:4b AS and SO

The expression, **as ... as**, is used when making affirmative statements. **So ... as** is used in negative statements.

**Affirmative:**   The meals in the cafeteria are **as** good **as** those served in the diner down the street.

Negative: The meals in the cafeteria are not **so** good **as** those served in the diner down the street.

**Never Say:** The meals in the cafeteria are **equally as** good **as** those served in the diner down the street. (This is redundant. The **equally** should be omitted.)

**4:4c** IS WHERE, IS WHEN, IS BECAUSE

Do not use these adverbial clauses in place of a noun or a noun phrase.

**Wrong:** Indexing **is where** you arrange files in alphabetical or numerical order.

**Right:** Indexing **is the arrangement** of files in alphabetical or numerical order.

**Wrong:** Follow-up **is when** you file material so it will be brought to someone's attention at a certain date.

**Right:** Follow-up **is a method** of filing material so it will be brought to someone's attention at a certain date.

When you begin a thought with "The reason is" or "The reason was," **follow it by a noun or noun clause introduced by that.** The use of **the reason was because** is redundant.

**Wrong:** I couldn't go to the show; **the reason was because** I had to work late.

**Right:** I couldn't go to the show **because** I had to work late.

or

The **reason** I couldn't go to the show was **that** I had to work late.

**4:4d** The Split Infinitive

Ordinarily, the infinitive should be kept intact, but the split infinitive is not considered a major fault and it is sometimes necessary in order to keep your meaning clear. Whether to split or not to split depends upon whether the sentence sounds awkward or the meaning is distorted.

| | |
|---|---|
| Awkward: | He asked me **to immediately write** the letter. |
| Improved: | He asked me **to write** the letter **immediately**. |
| Split but Clear: | I've scheduled your appointment **to just precede** the meeting. |
| Confusing: | I've scheduled your appointment **just to precede** the meeting. |
| Impossible: | I've scheduled your appointment **to precede just** the meeting. |

### 4:4e The Terminal Preposition

Here again, grammatical correctness must sometimes give way to the possibility of awkwardness or confusion. The original reason for the rule about never ending a sentence with a preposition was that a sentence should never be ended with a weak word. While this rule is observed to some extent in written sentences, it is usually overlooked in spoken language. For example, the following sentence reads better when it is ended with a noun, but it sounds more natural with the preposition at the end.

| | |
|---|---|
| Written: | We have no material on hand **with** which to fill your order. |
| Spoken: | We have no material on hand to fill your order **with**. |

A question also sounds better when it is ended with a preposition.

| | |
|---|---|
| Awkward: | **For** what are you waiting? |
| Better: | What are you waiting **for**? |

Sometimes there is no other way to end a sentence except with a preposition: The speaker was jeered **at**.

### 4:5 ACHIEVING SENTENCE COORDINATION

Sentence coordination means using similar constructions to express similar ideas.

- She likes **to read** and **to play** the stereo.
- She likes **reading** and **playing** the stereo.

Your speech will improve if you remember this rule of usage and avoid awkward combinations: She likes **to read** and **playing** the stereo.

## 4:5a Parallelism

The technical term for sentence coordination is **parallelism**. This involves matching phrases, clauses, and active or passive verbs.

Awkward: She bought a dress **with a pleated skirt** and **having a cowl neckline.**

Clear: She bought a dress **with a pleated skirt** and (with) **a cowl neckline.** (The word **with** does not need to be repeated, as it is understood.)

Awkward: If they **want** promotions, more initiative **must be shown** by them.

Clear: If they **want** promotions, they **must show** more initiative.

## 4:5b Partial Parallelism

When you are describing something in a series of three, **make sure that the sentence elements are in parallel form.**

Awkward: The play was **exciting, colorful, and had a good cast.**

Clear: The play was **exciting, colorful, and well-cast.**

## 4:5c Misleading Parallelism

The parallel structure should not be used for sentence elements which are unequal in kind or importance.

Awkward: **For his sake, for a sandwich and a cup of coffee,** I will help him.

Clear: **For his sake,** I will help him **with a sandwich and a cup of coffee.**

Awkward: **They went** to the conference and **they had a** rented limousine.

Clear: **They went** to the conference **in a** rented limousine.

**4:5d** False Parallelism

Expressions which should not be parallel are often put in parallel order unnecessarily.

Awkward:   Mr. Knight is **in his office** and **working** on the project.

Clear:     Mr. Knight is **in his office, working** on the project.

The conjunction **and** can simply be eliminated to produce a construction that is smoother and more straightforward.

**4:5e** Consistency in Parallelism

Words used in parallel structure must be the same parts of speech and must stand for comparable ideas.

Awkward:   Mr. Lawrence's assistant is **good-looking** and has a fine **education.**

Clear:     Mr. Lawrence's assistant is **good-looking** and **well-educated.**

Awkward:   Miss Manners thinks her **work** is more important than the **bookkeeper.**

Clear:     Miss Manners thinks her **work** is more important than **that of the bookkeeper.**
                  **or**
          Miss Manners thinks her **work** is more important than the bookkeeper's (work).

In the last sentence, the second **work** is not spoken but is understood.

**4:6** ELIMINATING SUPERFLUOUS WORDS

Many people use language that is grammatically correct but tiresome. They overload their sentences with unnecessary words and phrases that cause the attention of their listeners to wander. This is particularly unfortunate in business conversation, where you should get directly to the point.

**4:6a** THE FACT THAT

This is an expression you can usually do without.

| | |
|---|---|
| Wordy: | **Owing to the fact that** the shipment was delayed, we could not keep the delivery date. |
| Direct: | **Because** the shipment was delayed, we could not keep the delivery date. |
| Wordy: | **In spite of the fact that** we are shorthanded, we expect to complete the job on time. |
| Direct: | **Although** we are shorthanded, we expect to complete the job on time. |
| Wordy: | Let me **call your attention to the fact that** payment is a month overdue. |
| Direct: | Let me **remind you** that payment is a month overdue. |

**4:6b** Other Usages to Avoid

| Avoid | Use |
|---|---|
| along the lines of | like |
| blue in color | blue |
| consequently | so |
| come in contact with | meet |
| different in character | different |
| during the time that | while |
| for the purpose of | to |
| for the reason that | since, because |
| furthermore | then |
| in many cases | often |
| in a hasty manner | hastily |
| in the event of | if |
| in the nature of | like, similar to |
| likewise | and |
| one and the same | the same |
| seems evident that | seems that |
| six in number | six |
| there is no doubt but that | no doubt |
| with the result that | so that |

## CONCLUSION

Remember the three C's: clarity, coordination, and conciseness. You can't speak well without them.

## CHART I: PRONUNCIATION REMINDER

Here is a list of commonly mispronounced words in everyday use. You can make up a similar chart of words with which you have difficulty, along with their correct pronunciations.

### Adjectives

| | |
|---|---|
| amateur | AM-uh-tur |
| chic | sheek |
| genuine | GEN-yoo-inn |
| miniature | MIN-ee-uh-choor |
| robust | ro-BUST |
| sacrilegious | sak-ruh-LIH-jus |

### Nouns

| | |
|---|---|
| accessory | ak-SES-saw-ree |
| apricot | APP-rih-caht |
| experiment | ek-SPEHR-uh-ment |
| italics | ih-TAL-iks |
| radiator | RAY-dee-ay-tur |
| theater | THEE-uh-tur |

### Verbs

| | |
|---|---|
| bisect | bye-SEKT |
| hypnotize | HIP-nuh-tize |
| menstruate | MEN-stroo-ate |
| plagiarize | PLAY-juh-rize |
| route | root |
| surprise | surr-PRIZE |

## CHART II: SYNONYMS TO REMEMBER

Instead of using the same descriptive words all the time, vary your speech occasionally with an appropriate synonym. Make your own list of words that you use frequently, along with suitable synonyms for alternate uses, but always check on the meaning of the synonym to make sure that it fits your purpose.

| Instead of: | Sometimes Use: |
|---|---|
| beautiful | lovely |
| bright | brilliant |
| business | occupation |
| continual | incessant |
| delicious | luscious |
| difficult | arduous |
| example | archetype |
| fear | apprehension |
| grief | anguish |
| happy | jovial |
| hide | secrete |
| knowledge | erudition |
| large | gigantic |
| miserly | avaricious |
| necessary | requisite |
| rare | unique |
| sad | dejected |
| usual | habitual |
| violent | furious |

# Part 2

# EFFECTIVE LETTERS

# 5. GRAMMAR SIMPLIFIED

There is only one genuine rule of grammar: There are no hard and fast rules. Any construction that is used often enough and widely enough automatically becomes right and proper. Nevertheless, there are certain principles that should be observed, like the agreement of subject and verb or agreement of a pronoun with the word it represents.

A famous writer, like Jane Austen, can indulge in an occasional mistake of this kind, following a singular noun with a plural pronoun: "**Everybody** has a way of **their** own."

A secretary cannot afford such indulgence.

## 5:1 THREE SIMPLE PRINCIPLES

A secretary should adhere to the following principles since the letters written by a secretary reflect the character of the firm for which he or she works.

### 5:1a Agreement of Subject and Verb

It is obvious that a singular subject takes a singular verb, and a plural subject takes a plural verb.

- **Mary has** a headache.
- Her **headaches have become** chronic.

Not all sentences are as simple as these, however. Here are a few samples of more complex constructions that may cause confusion.

### 1. Alternative Subjects

Alternative subjects are usually separated by **or** or **nor**, and the verb takes its number from the subject nearest it.

- Neither the chart nor the **graphs are** suitable for our use.

### 2. Collective Nouns

A collective noun, like **board** or **committee,** is considered singular and takes a singular verb.

- The **board has** decided to postpone action on the measure.

### 3. Compound Subject

Two or more subjects in the third person, joined by **and,** take a plural verb.

- Mr. Jones **and** Mr. Kane **are** out of town.

### 4. Separation of Subject and Verb

The verb must agree with the subject, in spite of any separation by another noun or nouns.

- The **president**, with his aides and staff, **is** arriving tomorrow at noon.

### 5. Subordinate Clause

The verb in a subordinate clause agrees in number with the subject of the clause, not the subject of the sentence.

- The meeting is one of **those** that **are** scheduled for Wednesday mornings.

### 6. Subject That Follows the Verb

When the subject follows the verb, the verb and the subject still take the same number.

- In this type of desk **are** three convenient **drawers.**

### 7. Subject and Predicate Nominative

The predicate nominative follows the verb, but the verb still agrees with the subject in number, because the predicate is subordinate to the subject.

- The **error** in your order **is** the measurements.
- Production **costs are** the cause of the price increase.

### 8. Singular Subjects Plural in Form
Subjects like **economics, news,** and **politics,** which are plural in form but singular in meaning, use singular verbs.

- Today the **news is** good.
- The **economics** of the situation **is** in question.

### 9. Singular Pronouns
Singular pronouns take singular verbs, even when a phrase intervenes.

- **Everybody is** going to be there.
- **Each** of us **has** contributed to the fund.
- **Someone** always **meets** visitors at the airport.
- **One** of them **is** responsible.

### 10. Quantities or Numbers
A subject plural in form, which indicates a quantity or number, takes a singular verb when the subject is a unit in itself.

- **Twenty-five dollars is** too much to ask.
- **Three quarts is** sufficient.

**5:1b** Agreement of Pronoun and Antecedent

A pronoun always agrees, in all respects, with the word for which it stands.

1. A pronoun always agrees in number with the word for which it stands.

- A **man** should remove **his** hat in the elevator.
- **Men** should remove **their** hats in the elevator.

2. **Everyone** and **everybody** are singular nouns and should take singular pronouns.

- **Everyone** is going to wear **her** formal dress to the Christmas party.

3. A pronoun agrees with the nearer of two antecedents.

- Neither the desk nor the filing **cabinets** are up to **their** usual standard.

4. A collective noun takes either a singular or plural pronoun, depending on the meaning of the sentence. Here the word **committee** is considered as a unit:

● The **committee** decided to continue **its** discussions.

Here the members are acting individually:

● The **committee** stopped to order **their** lunches.

## 5:1c Correct Choice of Gender

A pronoun always agrees in gender with the word for which it stands.

● A **secretary** should not leave **her** telephone unattended.

● **Secretaries** should not leave **their** telephones unattended.

● An **executive** is expected to be at **his** desk promptly.

● **Executives** are expected to be at **their** desks promptly.

When, as in the above instances, the gender may be in doubt, the plural pronoun takes care of itself with the all-inclusive **their**. In the other two sentences you may have a problem, because there are certainly many male secretaries and female executives. The easiest way to overcome this difficulty is to use the plural whenever possible. If you do use the singular, then you must say:

● A **secretary** should not leave **his** or **her** telephone unattended.

● An **executive** is expected to be at **his** or **her** desk promptly.

Until recently, **his** was considered to include both sexes, but that usage seems old-fashioned today. You would not write the following sentence unless you were referring to an all-male group:

● **Everyone** is expected to improve **his** performance.

Instead you would write:

● **Everyone** is expected to improve **his** or **her** performance.

It may look awkward, but that construction will have to do until a new, all-inclusive pronoun is devised.

## 5:2 EIGHT PARTS OF SPEECH AND HOW TO USE THEM

Words are divided into parts of speech according to the thoughts they communicate and the ways in which they communicate them. They can be separated into five groups:

| | |
|---|---|
| **Nouns and Pronouns:** | words that name |
| **Adjectives and Adverbs:** | words that modify |
| **Prepositions and Conjunctions:** | words that connect |
| **Hybrid Words:** | words that can function in more than one capacity |
| **Verbs:** | words that assert |

### 5:2a Nouns and Pronouns

A noun names a person (**Jane**), place (**Los Angeles**), or thing (**telephone**). A noun can also represent a quality (**beauty**), idea (**dream**), or action (**speed**). A noun can be distinguished by its position in a sentence as a subject before the verb, an object after the verb, and an object of a preposition. It can also be used as a modifier with the addition of **'s**.

1. **Subject:**   The **invoice** was mailed yesterday.
2. **Object:**   I mailed you the **invoice** yesterday.
   I attached the invoice to my **letter**.
3. **Modifier:**   The **book's** cover was damaged in transit.
   **Mr. Jones's** records are in the file.

Pronouns are words that are used in place of nouns. They consist of four principal groups:

1. **Demonstrative:**   this, these, that, those
2. **Relative:**   who, whom, which, what, that, whose (**which** and **that** refer to things; **who** and **whom** refer to people.)
3. **Interrogative:**   who? which? what? whom? whose?
4. **Personal:**   I, you, we, he, she, it, they, me, us, him, his, her, their

Personal pronouns have been demonstrated by tests to be the toughest problem in English for the average person. There is often confusion over the use of the nominative, objective, and possessive cases. Test yourself:

## Personal Pronoun Test

1. She can complete the job faster than (I, me).
2. I do not have as much authority as (he, him).
3. It was a confidential matter between you and (she, her).
4. Everyone was present except (they, them).
5. No one but (he, him) had any difficulty passing the test.
6. We have considered everyone else for the position except (she, her).
7. I wish Mr. Cromwell's brother were more like (he, him).
8. You are ahead of Ruth and (I, me) in seniority.
9. What would the company do without (we, us) secretaries?
10. (We, Us) secretaries are indispensable.
11. Each department has (its, it's) own system.
12. The final choice is (yours, your's).

## Tips for the Correct Answers

1. After **as** and **than**, finish the sentence to discover the correct pronouns.
2. After prepositions, use the objective form of the pronoun: **me, him, her, us**, and **them**.
3. After any form of the verb **to be**, use the nominative form of the pronoun: **I, he, she, we**, and **they**.
4. When you have a double form, use the pronoun alone and the answer will be obvious: You are ahead of (I, me) in seniority.
5. When a pronoun is the subject of a sentence, use the nominative form.
6. Personal pronouns form the possessive by adding **s**.

**5:2b** Adjectives and Adverbs

An adjective modifies a noun and makes its meaning more exact. There are three general types of adjectives: **descriptive, limiting,** and **proper.**

1. **Descriptive:**    a **red** hat, a **hard** task, a **broken** pen
2. **Limiting:**    the **seventh** day, our **former** address, **several** choices
3. **Proper:**    the **British** rights, an **Italian** import

Many descriptive adjectives change their forms to indicate degree: **good, better, best.** A common problem in the use of adjectives is the confusion of the comparative with the superlative degree in sentences like these:

**Wrong:**    I paid the **largest** of the two bills.
**Right:**    I paid the **larger** of the two bills.

Most adjectives end in **er** for the comparative degree and in **est** for the superlative. The comparative degree refers to two persons or things. The superlative refers to more than two.

**Wrong:**    I have tried all of the machines and this one is **easier** to handle.
**Right:**    I have tried all of the machines and this one is **easiest** to handle.

Some adjectives do not lend themselves to the **er** and **est** endings, in which case they are combined with **more** or **most.**

- I wish you would be **more cautious.**

- She was the **most qualified** applicant.

Adverbs modify verbs, adjectives, or other adverbs. In the following instances, **almost, very,** and **faintly** are the adverbs:

**Verb:**    The telephone bell **rang faintly.**
**Adjective:**    We are **almost ready** to open.
**Adverb:**    We can deliver **very fast.**

One way in which adverbs can be distinguished from corresponding adjectives is by the ending **ly.**

| Adjective | Adverb |
|-----------|--------|
| bad | badly |
| sure | surely |
| easy | easily |
| neat | neatly |
| temporary | temporarily |

Another method of discovering whether a word is an adverb is to ask the questions, "When?" "Where?" "How?" and "How much?" Words that answer any of these questions will almost always be adverbs.

| When? | now, early, late, yesterday |
|-------|------------------------------|
| Where? | here, there, above, below, far, near |
| How? | rapidly, slowly, asleep, awake |
| How Much? | often, seldom, partly, entirely |

Some adverbs are compared by the addition of **more** or **most**, while others are compared by the endings **er** and **est**.

- She typed the contracts **more rapidly** than I did.
- This is the form we use **most often**.
- Our busy season is drawing near**er**.
- The near**est** airport is Kennedy.

## 5:2c Prepositions and Conjunctions

A preposition links a noun or pronoun with another word in the sentence.

- We expect to have the proposal ready **by** Friday.
- We wrote you **on** the thirtieth.
- I hope to hear **from** you soon.

Other commonly used prepositions are: **against, among, around, at, before , behind, below, between, beyond, during, for, in, like, of, since, to, until, with.**

Prepositions are often used in idiomatic phrases:

| comply with | different from |
|-------------|----------------|
| adapted to | listen to |
| angry with | plan to go |
| fond of | independent of |
| with regard to | due to |

The preposition should never be omitted when time is involved. This is a practice which should be avoided.

**Wrong:**  I shall write you again September 15th.
**Right:**  I shall write you again **on** September 15th.

**Wrong:**  We are closed Easter week.
**Right:**  We are closed **during** Easter week.

Conjunctions join words or groups of words in a sentence. When they join elements of equal grammatical rank, they are called **coordinating**. Your choice of a conjunction depends upon the exact meaning you want to convey.

| Meaning | Conjunction |
|---|---|
| Addition | and, both, also, too, further |
| Choice | either, or, neither, nor, else, otherwise |
| Contrast | but, yet, still, notwithstanding, however |
| Consequence | therefore, then, so, hence, consequently |

| | |
|---|---|
| **Addition:** | The contract **and** the check are enclosed. |
| **Choice:** | **Neither** the contract **nor** the check was enclosed. |
| **Contrast:** | The contract was enclosed **but** the check was not. |
| **Consequence:** | The contract has been signed, **so** I am returning it to you. |

The so-called **subordinating** conjunction joins dependent clauses to main clauses. Subordinate conjunctions can be grouped according to the meaning of the sentence.

| Meaning | Conjunction |
|---|---|
| Time | as, while, until, before, since, after |
| Reason | as, whereas, because, for, since |
| Condition | if, unless, except, otherwise |
| Comparison | as, according, as far as, so |

| | |
|---|---|
| **Time:** | Mr. Atkins will arrive **before** the convention begins. |
| **Reason:** | We are moving **because** our lease has expired. |
| **Condition:** | We shall have to foreclose **if** we do not hear from you by the first of the month. |
| **Comparison:** | Mr. Atkins will be free all morning, **as far as** I know. |

## 5:2d Hybrids

Some words become different parts of speech according to the way they are used. When verbs become nouns they are called **gerunds** and they are used exactly like nouns. They always end in **ing** and are often preceded by possessive nouns.

- Her **going** to lunch early was inconvenient.
- His **writing** the letter saved a phone call.
- **Smoking** is not permitted in the dining room.

Nouns become adjectives when they are used as possessives.

- The **executives'** washroom
- The **ladies'** lounge

In modern parlance, nouns are sometimes used as adjectives without the addition of **'s** or **s'**.

- The item comes in four **decorator** colors.
- We have a complete line of **designer** sportswear.

Nouns, pronouns, adverbs, and adjectives become interjections when they are used as exclamations.

- **Goodness!**
- **My!**
- **Well!**
- **Beautiful!**

Certain nouns and verbs are used interchangeably, and the only way to tell which part of speech they are is by the way they are used.

- I think we will be able to **effect** a settlement. (verb)
- We are feeling the **effect** of the recession. (noun)

## 5:2e Verbs

The verb is the most essential word in a sentence. In fact, a sentence can be constructed containing only a verb.

- Go.
- Come.

- Wait.
- Stop.

Verbs are classified according to what is known as **voice**. Active voice means that the subject performs the action. Passive voice means that the subject receives the action. Sentences in active voice always have a stronger effect.

| | |
|---|---|
| **Active**: | We **wrote** the letter yesterday. |
| **Passive**: | The letter **was written** yesterday. |
| | |
| **Active**: | He **asked** us to reply. |
| **Passive**: | We **were asked** to reply. |

There are four ways to identify the verb in a sentence. The verb is the word that denotes an action, a happening, a fulfillment, or a condition.

| | |
|---|---|
| **Action**: | The stock market **crashed**. |
| **Happening**: | It **occurred** in 1929. |
| **Fulfillment**: | We **succeeded** in our attempts to find a new formula. |
| **Condition**: | Prices **are** rising. |

See how many verbs you can recognize in the following test:

### Verb Recognition Test

Dear Mr. Yates:

We hope you have set aside the week of May 14 in order to attend the Dealers Convention to be held in Atlanta this year.

The seminars will be held at the Biltmore Hotel, and sessions will start each morning at nine o'clock in the Peachtree Room. Lunch will be served in the Georgian Terrace from twelve until two. After two, you are free for relaxation, and evening entertainment has been arranged.

The cost of the entire week, including transportation by American Airlines from Boston to Atlanta, will be $695.00. The plane will leave Logan International Airport on May 14 at 8 A.M. If you are interested, please fill in the attached reservation form and return it to us. No reservations will be accepted after May 1.

We know you will find your stay enjoyable as well as productive, and we look forward to seeing you.

Sincerely,

How many verbs were you able to identify? Eighteen would be perfect, fifteen would be good, and a score of below fifteen shows that you have trouble identifying verbs. (The answers are at the end of this chapter.)

## 5:3 SIX BASIC TENSES THAT ARE ALL YOU NEED TO KNOW

Verbs exist in six basic tenses, the purpose of which is to indicate the three divisions of time: past, present, and future.

**Present Tense**

This tense indicates that the action or condition is going on, or exists, now.

- We **know** you will find your stay enjoyable as well as productive, and we **look** forward to seeing you.

**Past Tense**

The past tense indicates that the action or condition took place, or existed, at some definite time in the past.

- We hope you **found** your stay enjoyable as well as productive.

**Future Tense**

This tense is an indication that the action or condition will take place, or exist, sometime in the future.

- The seminars **will be held** at the Biltmore Hotel and sessions **will start** each morning at nine.

The future may also be indicated by the present tense when it is followed by a phrase concerning time.

- He **is going** to the convention tomorrow.

**Present Perfect Tense**

The present perfect tense covers an action or condition begun in the past and completed in the present.

- After two, you are free for relaxation, and evening entertainment **has been arranged**.

**Past Perfect Tense**

This tense covers an action or condition completed in the past.

- We found that evening entertainment **had been arranged**.

### Future Perfect Tense

This tense indicates that an action or condition will be completed, or will exist, in the future.

- The first seminar **will have concluded** before you arrive.

Most people learn to use the appropriate tenses when they are children, long before they know the names that grammarians have given them. The only tense that is a bit tricky is the future perfect. Be careful not to omit the **have**.

**Wrong**: On Monday, he will be gone for two weeks.
**Right**: On Monday, he will **have** been gone for two weeks.

## 5:4 THOSE DECEPTIVE SOUND-ALIKE WORDS

In English there are a number of words that sound so much alike that you may be tempted to use one for the other. Be careful of this, for the meanings are usually quite different.

| | |
|---|---|
| accept | to receive |
| except | to exclude |
| ad | abbreviation of **advertisement** |
| add | to make an addition |
| adapt | to adjust |
| adopt | to accept |
| advice | counsel (noun) |
| advise | to counsel or notify (verb) |
| affect | to influence or to pretend |
| effect | to bring about (verb) |
| | result (noun) |
| all ready | prepared |
| already | by this time |
| altogether | entirely |
| all together | all of us or all of you |
| appraise | to estimate |
| apprise | to notify |

| | |
|---|---|
| ascent | the act of rising |
| assent | consent |
| | |
| biannual | twice a year |
| biennial | once in two years |
| | |
| bloc | a group |
| block | to stop |
| | |
| canvas | coarse cloth |
| canvass | to solicit |
| | |
| capital | a city |
| capitol | a building |
| | |
| cite | to quote |
| site | location |
| | |
| compliment | an expression of admiration |
| complement | complete |
| | |
| communicable | able to be transmitted |
| communicative | willing to convey ideas |
| | |
| consul | an official |
| council | an advisory group |
| counsel | advice |
| | |
| continual | often repeated |
| continuous | uninterrupted |
| | |
| credible | believable |
| credulous | easily convinced |
| creditable | worthy of praise |
| | |
| deprecate | to show disapproval |
| depreciate | to lower in value |
| | |
| disinterested | impartial |
| uninterested | lacking interest |
| | |
| dialect | regional speech |
| dialogue | conversation between two or more parties |

| | |
|---|---|
| emigrate | to leave a country or locality |
| immigrate | to enter a country or locality |
| | |
| every one | used when followed by **of** |
| everyone | everybody |
| | |
| farther | refers to distance |
| further | refers to time, quantity, or degree |
| | |
| formally | in a formal way |
| formerly | previously |
| | |
| guarantee | to promise or to secure |
| guaranty | a pledge of performance |
| | |
| healthful | giving health |
| healthy | having health |
| | |
| in | denotes location |
| into | movement from without to within |
| in to | indicates direction |
| | |
| lay | to set down or deposit |
| lie | to recline or rest |
| lay | past tense of **lie** |
| | |
| limit | a boundary |
| limitation | a restriction |
| | |
| meanwhile | during an intervening time (adverb) |
| meantime | an interval (noun) |
| | |
| moral | proper or good |
| morale | the attitude of a group |
| | |
| official | holding a position of authority |
| officious | offering unwanted advice |
| | |
| principal | chief, main (adjective) |
| | the leader (noun) |
| principle | a basic law or fact |
| | |
| persecute | to harass |
| prosecute | to bring legal proceedings |

| | |
|---|---|
| personal | private |
| personnel | a group of employees |
| practical | successfully put into practice |
| practicable | capable of being put into practice |
| precede | to come before |
| proceed | to carry onward |
| prescription | an order for dispensing medicine |
| proscription | a prohibition |
| somebody | an unspecified person |
| someone | some person |
| some one | a particular person |
| sometime | on some occasion |
| some time | a span of time |
| stationary | in a fixed position |
| stationery | writing materials |
| stricture | severe criticism |
| structure | something constructed |
| their | possessive pronoun |
| there | at a certain place |
| they're | contraction of **they are** |
| vice | a defect or bad habit |
| vise | a clamp |
| waive | to give up |
| wave | a swell |

## 5:5 WORDS THAT ARE TWINS, BUT NOT IDENTICAL

The following words are very similar in meaning, but there are hairline differences.

| | |
|---|---|
| ability | the power of accomplishment |
| capacity | the ability to hold or absorb |

| | |
|---|---|
| advise | to counsel or warn |
| inform | to tell or communicate |
| | |
| among | refers to more than two |
| between | refers to only two |
| | |
| amount | a sum or total |
| number | a group of individual parts |
| | |
| average | typical, commonplace |
| normal | conforming to a typical pattern or type |
| | |
| usual | customary |
| ordinary | commonly encountered |
| | |
| balance | refers to financial matters |
| remainder | leftovers |
| | |
| can | implies ability |
| may | requests permission |
| | |
| common | belonging to two or more |
| mutual | something given and received |
| | |
| compare | point out likeness or difference |
| contrast | distinguish differences |
| | |
| convince | overcome doubts |
| persuade | influence to action |
| | |
| extract | to obtain or pull out |
| excerpt | to select or take out |
| | |
| fewer | refers to numbers |
| less | indicates amount |
| | |
| imply | to suggest something |
| infer | to draw a conclusion |
| | |
| latter | the second of two persons or things |
| last | the final of more than two |
| | |
| shall | first person, simple future |
| | second and third persons, determination |

| | |
|---|---|
| will | second and third persons, simple future |
| | first person, determination |

**Example:**

**I shall** attend the seminar. (simple future)
**She shall** be rewarded. (determination)

**He will** attend the seminar. (simple future)
**I will** see that it is done.
(determination)

| | |
|---|---|
| that | a defining or restrictive pronoun |
| which | a nondefining, nonrestrictive pronoun |

**Example:**

The machine **that** is broken is in the repair shop. (tells which machine)

The machine, **which** is broken, is in the repair shop. (explains a fact about the machine)

## ANSWERS TO TESTS

### Personal Pronoun Test

| | |
|---|---|
| 1. I | 7. him |
| 2. he | 8. me |
| 3. her | 9. us |
| 4. them | 10. we |
| 5. him | 11. its |
| 6. her | 12. yours |

### Verb Recognition Test

| | |
|---|---|
| **First Paragraph:** | hope |
| | have set |
| | to attend |
| **Second Paragraph:** | to be held |
| | will be held |
| | will start |
| | will be served |
| | are |
| | has been arranged |

| | |
|---|---|
| **Third Paragraph:** | will be |
| | will leave |
| | are |
| | fill in |
| | return |
| | will be accepted |
| **Fourth Paragraph:** | know |
| | will find |
| | look |
| | (**seeing** is a gerund) |

## CONCLUSION

Most grammatical principles are as simple as the operation of a typewriter, and as easy to master once you make up your mind.

# 6. QUICK AND EASY PUNCTUATION

Punctuation was not invented until the fifteenth century, but the twentieth-century secretary cannot function without it. You can judge whether you are using punctuation correctly by rereading a letter you have just written. If you get out of breath before the end of a sentence, you have used too little punctuation. If the effect is halting and uneven, perhaps you used too many commas—a common mistake.

## 6:1 SECRETS OF COMMA PLACEMENT

The first secret in comma placement is the reliable rule of three, sometimes referred to as the **serial comma**.

### 6:1a Rule of Three

In a series of three or more items with a single conjunction, use a comma after each item preceding the conjunction.

- I opened the letter, read it, and informed Mr. Ames of its contents.
- We interview applicants on Mondays, Wednesdays, and Fridays.

**Exception:** The last comma is often omitted in the names of business firms.

- Batten, Barton, Durstine & Osborn, Inc.
- Manning, Selvage & Lee/Chicago, Inc.

**6:1b** With Nonessential Phrases

A nonessential phrase that is inserted by way of comment should be marked off with commas.

- Mr. Albert Baynes, **whom you met last summer**, has been appointed head of the committee.

The sentence would still make sense without the section enclosed by commas.

**Exception:** Do not use a comma before **of** in a phrase indicating place or position.

- Mr. Albert Baynes **of** Baynes and Company has been appointed head of the committee.

**6:1c** Before BUT or AND

Place a comma before **and, but, for, or,** and **nor** when they join two independent clauses, unless the clauses are very short.

- We received your letter, **but** the merchandise has not yet arrived.
- I am glad you called the matter to my attention, **for** it is my job to serve you.
- The meeting is important **and** I plan to attend.

**6:1d** For the Sake of Clarity

A comma break is sometimes necessary in order to make your meaning perfectly clear.

- For as little as twenty-five dollars you can buy a complete makeup kit, or a one-ounce bottle of perfume and a four-ounce container of spray cologne.

The comma before the perfume and spray items indicates that they go together.

- Whenever practicable, action should be taken to facilitate speedier delivery.

Introductory clauses should always be followed by a comma to avoid confusion.

### 6:1e Before and After Quotations

Commas should be placed before or after quotations that are incorporated into the sentence.

- The speaker said, "We must increase production if we want to increase profits."
- "We must increase production," the speaker said, "if we want to increase profits."
- "We must increase production," the speaker said.

**Inside or Outside?** Unlike the man with the long beard, who didn't know whether to sleep with his beard inside or outside the covers, the secretary has a definite rule to follow: The comma is **always** placed **inside** the quotation marks.

### 6:1f Guarding Against Four Common Errors

Here are some cautions for the secretary who uses too many commas.

1. Do not separate a verb and the phrase that completes the sentence.

**Wrong:** We asked, for an extension.
The product we are featuring, is called Zanadu.
**Right:** We asked for an extension.
The product we are featuring is called Zanadu.

2. Do not use a comma after a simple conjunction like **but** or **and**.

**Wrong:** We like your idea **but,** the consensus is that it would not work for us.
**Right:** We like your idea, but the consensus is that it would not work for us.

3. Do not use a comma to separate two words joined by **and**.

**Wrong:** She has ability, **and** integrity.
**Right:** She has ability **and** integrity.

4. Do not use a comma before a title unless it is in quotes.

**Wrong:** The name of the book is, **Complete Book of Business Etiquette.**

**Right**: The name of the book is **Complete Book of Business Etiquette**.

The name of the article is, "Business Etiquette."

## 6:2 WHERE TO USE THE SEMICOLON

The semicolon is used as a mark of division that is more emphatic than a comma, but not as forceful as a period. The semicolon has four definite uses that should be easy to remember.

### 6:2a To Separate Related Clauses

When related clauses are not separated by a conjunction, a semicolon should be used in its place.

- Please remit at once; the bill is long overdue.

When related clauses are lengthy, even if they are separated by a conjunction, the semicolon should be used, especially if the clauses already contain commas.

- The first job we have open involves drawing up charts and graphs, and typing reports; while the second requires some familiarity with legal documents, court papers, and legal citations.

### 6:2b To Separate Listed Items

Place semicolons between elements in a series which contain several words apiece, or elements already punctuated by commas.

- We have branches in Albany, New York; Hartford, Connecticut; and Springfield, Massachusetts.
- We interview applicants on Mondays from ten to twelve; on Wednesdays from one to three; and all day Friday.

### 6:2c Before Conjunctive Adverbs

Use a semicolon before an adverb that acts as a conjunction, such as **accordingly**, **also**, **besides**, **consequently**, **however**,

**nevertheless**, **otherwise**, and **therefore**. The semicolon serves to emphasize the importance of the following clause.

- You placed your order soon enough; **however**, an unexpected shortage has caused a delay.
- We were pleased with the samples you sent; **therefore**, we would like to place an order.

**6:2d** Before THAT IS and NAMELY

Use a semicolon to separate two clauses when the second clause begins with **namely** or **that is**.

- We would like to hear from you in greater detail regarding your background; **that is**, with a résumé of your education, experience, and salary expectations.

**6:3** THE PERIOD

The period has three uses, none of which is very complicated.
1. At the end of a declarative or imperative sentence:

- Your suggestions were very helpful. (declarative)
- Do not proceed until you hear from us. (imperative)

2. After initials and abbreviations, except those used as symbols, like CBS, CIA, or two-letter state abbreviations, like CA, IL, and NY.

Ms.
D.D.S.
a.m.
E.S.T.
Eliz.

**Exceptions**: Do not use a period after shortened forms for proper names, or after contractions of common words.

Joe
Abe
memo
photo
Ass'n
math

3. A period is used after each letter or number in an outline or list, unless the letter or number is enclosed in parentheses. Do not use a period after 1st, 2nd, or 3rd, or similar contractions.

> 3.
> IV.
> (5)
> 6th

## 6:4 APOSTROPHES AND WHERE TO PUT THEM

Apostrophes have three uses:

1. To show possession
2. To indicate omission
3. To indicate the plural of figures, letters, and words mentioned as words

### 6:4a To Show Possession

This is the most complicated use of the apostrophe, and it causes the most confusion. There are seven rules for this application, the first of which is the simplest.

1. Use an **apostrophe** and **s** to form the possessive of a noun not ending in **s**.

   > men's
   > women's
   > secretary's
   > executive's

2. Use an **apostrophe alone** to form the possessive of a plural noun ending in **s**.

   > secretaries'
   > executives'
   > employees'

3. Use an **apostrophe** and **s**, or the apostrophe alone, to form the possessive of a singular noun ending in **s**.

   > the boss's desk
   > Miss Jones' office

4. Add an **apostrophe** and **s** to the second member of a pair to indicate joint possession.

- We buy our stationery at Benson and Hedge's.
- We use Smith and Dale's office supplies.

5. Add an **apostrophe** and **s** to the last word in a compound.

> somebody else's fault
> his father-in-law's business

6. The **apostrophe** and **s** are used in the possessive case of indefinite pronouns such as **one, no one, somebody, nobody, someone,** or **another**.

> somebody's responsibility
> one's day off

7. Never use an apostrophe with the possessive **its** or with **hers, his, yours, theirs, ours,** or **whose**.

| | |
|---|---|
| **Wrong:** | What is **it's** significance? |
| | **Who's** turn is it? |
| **Right:** | What is **its** significance? |
| | **Whose** turn is it? |

## **6:4b** To Indicate Omission

Use an apostrophe to indicate the omission of figures or letters.

> won't
> doesn't
> haven't
> July '80

## **6:4c** To Indicate Certain Plurals

An **apostrophe** and **s** indicate the plural of figures, letters, and words in italics or boldface type.

- His 7's look like 4's.
- He doesn't dot his i's or cross his t's.

- Our business began in the 1940's.
- Your letter contains too many **and**'s.

## 6:5 THE BASIC USES OF COLONS

As every secretary knows, the basic business use of the colon is after the salutation of a letter.

Dear Mr. Wayne:
Dear Madam:

The next most important use is as an introduction to a list, an explanatory statement, or a long quotation.

- We wish to place our order for the following:
- These are the reasons for our product's popularity:
- The chairman then stated:

A colon is also used to indicate digital time, or to separate chapter and verse of a Biblical reference.

11:30 A.M.
Genesis 45:16

## 6:6 THE LIMITED USES OF DASHES

A secretary might pursue his or her entire career without having occasion to use a dash. The use of the dash usually depends upon the employer's taste in the matter. Dashes can take the place of commas, semicolons, and colons, where desired; but their use is preferably limited to marking an abrupt interruption in the thought of a sentence. The dash is formed with two hyphens, and no space should be left between it and the surrounding words.

- It was the packing--not the handling--that was responsible for the breakage.
- The price--I am sure you will agree--is lower than any we have offered so far.
- We have had a number of inquiries--I think there have been a dozen in the past week--concerning our new premium offer.

## 6:7 HOW TO HANDLE QUOTATION MARKS

There are three questions which arise in connection with quotation marks:

1. When to use them
2. Where to place punctuation in relation to them
3. Where to place quotation marks in quotes of more than one paragraph

### 6:7a When to Use Quotes

(1) Quotation marks are used when repeating directly and exactly what someone has said.

- The chairman said, "Our ratings have shown a satisfactory increase."

(2) Quotation marks are omitted when repeating words indirectly or inexactly.

- The chairman said that our ratings have shown an increase.

(3) Quotation marks are used to enclose slang or colloquialisms, when the rest of the letter uses more formal language.

- It is my opinion that the recommendations of the committee are so much "horsefeathers."

(4) The first time an unusual word or phrase is used, it should be put in quotes, but the quotes are not repeated the second time.

- This group of elderly citizens calls itself "The Gray Panthers." The Gray Panthers fight for equal rights for senior citizens.

### 6:7b Where to Place Other Punctuation

1. Commas and periods are placed inside the quotation marks.

- "I will fly on ahead," she said, "and make all the arrangements for your stay."

2. Colons and semicolons are placed outside quotation marks.

- These items are "hot": roller skates, running shoes, and skis.

- You ordered the shade called "French Taupe"; but the only shade available is "Tender Tan."

3. Question marks and exclamation marks are placed inside or outside the quotation mark, depending on whether or not they are a part of the quotation.

- She asked us, "Who is responsible for this mistake?"
- Who wrote "Elements of Style"?
- Tell them our answer is "Absolutely not!"
- Now he tells me, "I cannot possibly attend"!

**6:7c** Quotes of More Than One Paragraph

When you quote more than one paragraph, put quotation marks at the beginning of each paragraph and at the end of the last paragraph.

Dear Mr. Sweet:

On November 7, 1982, I received the following letter from Mr. Lawrence C. Conners of Conners and Doling:

"I have ready the copy of the covering letter addressed to you under date of October 30, 1982, wherein the Colonial Bank forwarded to you a check in the sum of $1,256.71, representing the final amount due from the Estate of William J. Donovan to the Estate of Harry Donovan.

"I am concerned with this distribution inasmuch as the check is not payable to any legal representative of Jessie Donovan.

"On November 1, 1982, I called the Colonial Bank and spoke with Mr. Charles D. Sweet, who is going to look into the matter."

Since I have heard nothing further from Mr. Conners, I would appreciate your bringing me up to date on the status of this case.

Sincerely,

## 6:8 12 EASY SOLUTIONS TO PUNCTUATION PROBLEMS

Most punctuation problems have easy solutions. Here are a dozen typical cases regarding periods, quotation marks, commas, and parentheses.

### 6:8a Periods

1. After an abbreviation, omit a second period when the abbreviation comes at the end of a sentence.

• The post office address is Albany, N.Y.

2. After sums of money in dollar denominations, omit the period unless cents are added.

• I enclose $50 for two orchestra tickets.

• The price is $7.50 a pound.

3. To indicate an omission from a sentence or quotation, use three periods in succession.

• He concluded his speech, "...and with your help we will succeed."

### 6:8b Quotation Marks

1. Quotation marks are used to enclose the titles of articles, books, brochures, operas, paintings, plays, motion pictures, poems, and songs, unless you type the titles in all caps. Do not use quotation marks with the names of well-known publications like Reader's Digest, or when mentioning the Bible or its books.

• I have reserved seats to "The Pirates of Penzance."

• The quotation comes from the book of Genesis.

2. Use single quotation marks to enclose a quotation within a quotation.

● The notice reads, "Please endorse your checks, 'Pay to the order of Bankers Trust.'"

3. Quotation marks always come in pairs. Remember to conclude with them when you have begun that way.

**Wrong:** "I like the progress you have made, he said.
**Right:** "I like the progress you have made," he said.

## 6:8c Commas

1. A quotation that flows right along with the sentence is not set off by commas.

● They raised their hands to indicate "Yes" or "No."

● The manager said that he would "reduce absenteeism by 20%."

In a date consisting of the month, the day, and the year, set off the year by commas. Omit the commas in a date consisting of only the month and the year.

● Our company was founded by John Bates on April 25, 1932.

● Our company was founded by John Bates in April 1932.

3. With four or more figures, use a comma before each three numbers.

3,987
39,870
398,705
3,987,050

## 6:8d Parentheses

1. Parentheses are used to differentiate between two cities of the same name. Do not use a comma before a parenthesis.

**Wrong:** The Springfield, (Mass.) General Hospital
**Right:** The Springfield (Mass.) General Hospital

2. Use parentheses to enclose figures that have been repeated to ensure accuracy.

- We pay two dollars ($2) for typewriter ribbons.
- We have had twenty-five (25) claims for damages.

3. Use a question mark in parentheses to indicate uncertainty.

- I believe the address is 1540(?) Broadway.

## 6:9 PUNCTUATION TEST

Here is a sample letter incorporating much of the use of punctuation covered in this chapter. See how well you can punctuate it, before checking with the answer that follows.

Dear Mrs Williams

By this time you must have received our letter read it and made a decision as to our proposition Mr Robert Graves whom you met when you were here is anxious to go ahead

Only this morning Mr Graves asked me have you heard from Mrs Williams and I had to reply No We would appreciate learning your answer it means a great deal to us As Mr Graves assistant I am as eager as he is to see the deal consummated Mr Graves has just taken over his father in laws real estate operations and he wants to maintain the firms fine reputation

To repeat our proposal the loft is priced at fifty thousand dollars $50000 and the monthly maintenance charge is $47550 We think its a good offer and we hope to hear from you soon

Sincerely

The letter retains paragraphing and capitalization, so that it will not be too difficult for you to punctuate. Go over it carefully, checking every possible comma, semicolon, apostrophe, period, and quotation mark. If you have absorbed the material in this chapter, you should make very few mistakes.

Answer to Punctuation Test

Dear Mrs. Williams:

By this time you must have received our letter, read it, and made a decision as to our proposition. Mr. Robert Graves, whom you met when you were here, is anxious to go ahead.

Only this morning, Mr. Graves asked me, "Have you heard from Mrs. Williams?" and I had to reply "No." We would appreciate learning your answer; it means a great deal to us. As Mr. Graves' assistant, I am as eager as he is to see the deal consummated. Mr. Graves has just taken over his father-in-law's real estate operations, and he wants to maintain the firm's fine reputation.

To repeat our proposal, the loft is priced at fifty thousand dollars ($50,000), and the monthly maintenance charge is $475.50. We think it's a good offer, and we hope to hear from you soon.

Sincerely,

## CONCLUSION

Punctuation is the lifeblood of the letter; do your part to keep it flowing.

# 7. HELPFUL SPELLING AIDS

The three most difficult spelling decisions a secretary must make are:

1. When to drop the final **e** before suffixes like **ing**, **ly**, **able**, and **ness**
2. When to double final consonants before **ing**, **ed**, **er**, or **est**
3. How to spell words using prefixes like **mis**, **dis**, and **un**

There are some helpful rules, on these and similar questions, that every secretary should know.

## 7:1 SIX PRIMARY RULES

The first rule to be considered is the rule of the silent **e**, which is said to cover more words than any other spelling rule.

### 7:1a The Silent E

A final silent **e** is usually dropped before a suffix like **able** that begins with a vowel, but it is retained before a suffix like **ness** or **ly** that begins with a consonant.

| | | |
|---|---|---|
| advise | advising | advisement |
| | advisable | |
| arrive | arrival | |
| | arriving | |
| bare | baring | barely, bareness |
| | | bareback |
| believe | believing | |
| | believable | |
| care | caring | careful, careless |
| | | carefree |
| excite | exciting | excitement |
| | excitable | |
| extreme | extremist | extremely |
| hope | hoping | hopeless |
| | | hopeful |
| like | likable | likeness |
| | | likely |
| live | livable | lively |
| | | livelihood |
| love | lovable | lovely |
| | | lovesick |
| move | movable | movement |
| owe | owing | |
| purchase | purchasing | |
| | purchasable | |
| safe | | safely, safety |
| | | safeguard |
| sincere | sincerity | sincerely |
| sure | | surely |
| | | surety |
| use | usable | useless |
| | usage | useful |

Like all rules, this one has certain exceptions.

**Exceptions:**

a. The silent **e** is retained when **ing** is added and dropping it would cause confusion with another word, as in **dye** and **dyeing**, which are not to be confused with **die** and **dying**, in which the final **e** in **die** has been changed to **y**.

b. The silent **e** is retained before a suffix beginning with a vowel in order to simplify pronunciation, as in **acre, acreage; here, herein; line, lineage; mile, mileage; there, therein.**

c. The silent **e** is dropped before a suffix beginning with a consonant in certain common words like **abridgment, acknowledgment, argument, awful, doubly, duly, incredibly, judgment, possibly, probably, truly, wholly.**

d. The silent **e** is retained in words ending with **ce** or **ge**, even when the suffix begins with a vowel, as in **advantageous, changeable, outrageous, noticeable,** and **serviceable.**

**7:1b** Double or Not

The rule for doubling final consonants can be divided into two parts.

1. Words of one syllable that end in a single consonant, preceded by a single vowel, double the consonant when followed by a suffix beginning with a vowel.

clan, clannish
drop, dropped, dropping
man, mannish, manned
plan, planned, planning, planner
red, redder, reddest, redden, reddish
run, running, runner

**Exception:** The letter **x** is never doubled.

fix, fixing, fixable, fixation
tax, taxes, taxing, taxable, taxation

2. Words of more than one syllable, accented on the last syllable and ending in a single consonant preceded by a single vowel, double the consonant when followed by a suffix beginning with a vowel.

      acquit, acquitted, acquitting, acquittal
      admit, admitted, admitting, admittance
      begin, beginner, beginning
      control, controlled, controller, controlling, controllable
      equip, equipped, equipping
      forget, forgetting, forgettable, unforgettable
      occur, occurred, occurring, occurrence
      overlap, overlapped, overlapping
      prefer, preferred, preferring
      refer, referred, referring, referral
      transfer, transferred, transferring

**Exceptions:**

a. If the accent changes to another syllable when the suffix is added, you do not double the final consonant.

      confer, conference
      defer, deference
      infer, inference
      prefer, preference, preferable

b. Words ending in a final consonant preceded by two vowels do not double the final consonant.

      appear, appeared, appearing, appearance
      reveal, revealed, revealing

c. Words ending in two consonants do not double the final consonant.

      insist, insisted, insistence, insistent
      invent, invented, inventor

d. Words not accented on the final syllable usually do not double the final consonant.

      credit, credited, creditor
      happen, happened, happening
      moisten, moistened, moistening

## 7:1c MIS, DIS, and UN

Words beginning with **mis** or **dis** offer so many opportunities for mistakes that they can baffle the most expert secretary. Take for example, **disappoint**. It often comes out: **dissappoint, disapoint,** or **dissapoint. Misspell** is another such word. Is it **mispell, misspel,** or **misppell?**

A good rule to remember is that only about forty common words begin with **diss** or **miss,** while closer to 400 words begin with **dis** or **mis.**

You will make fewer errors if you separate the prefix from the root word. Thus, in **disappoint,** the root word is **appoint,** so only one **s** is required. In **misspell** the root word is **spell,** so naturally there must be two **s**'s.

The prefix **un** follows the same formula. When the root word begins with **n,** there will be two **n**'s; when the root word begins with another letter, there will be one **n.**

unnatural, unnecessary, unnegotiable, unnoticed
unabridged, unavoidable, unconditional, unlimited

## 7:1d ABLE and IBLE

The primary rule for the **able/ible** quandary is that the ending should be **able** if the base is a complete word, and **ible** if the base is not a complete word.

| | |
|---|---|
| acceptable | fashionable |
| available | favorable |
| breakable | noticeable |
| comfortable | perishable |
| commendable | predictable |
| considerable | presentable |
| dependable | profitable |
| detectable | readable |
| discreditable | taxable |
| drinkable | workable |

| | |
|---|---|
| audible | incorrigible |
| collapsible | indelible |
| combustible | infallible |
| compatible | intelligible |
| credible | irresistible |
| divisible | negligible |
| edible | ostensible |
| eligible | plausible |
| feasible | tangible |
| forcible | visible |

Like all other grammatical rules, this one has a number of exceptions.

ABLE **Exceptions**:

a. The ending is **able** if the base word is a word that has dropped the final **e**, such as **believable, debatable, desirable, excitable, excusable, likable, presumable, sizable, and valuable.**

b. The ending is **able** if the base word ended in a **y** which has been changed to **i**, such as **classifiable, enviable, justifiable,** and **reliable.**

c. The ending should usually be **able** if the base ends in a hard **c** or a hard **g**, like the sound of **c** in **cut** or the **g** in **got**. Examples include **amicable, applicable, explicable, implacable, navigable, practicable, irrevocable.**

In the case of **able**, there are exceptions to the exceptions, and you will have to try to memorize words such as **equitable, inevitable, memorable, palpable,** and **vulnerable,** which follow no rule.

IBLE **Exceptions**:

a. The ending should usually be **ible** if the base can form another word with the addition of **ion** or **sion**. For example, **perfect-perfection-perfectible.** Other such words are **accessible, collectible, connectible, convertible, corruptible, digestible, reversible, suggestible.** Some words, like **detect**, are exceptions to the exception: **detect-detection-detectable.**

b. Some bases ending in **ss** have **ible** endings, even though they are complete words in themselves: **dismissible, accessible,** and **remissible.**

c. The ending should usually be **ible** if the base ends in a soft **c** like **reduce**, or a soft **g** like **intelligent**. Examples are **eligible, forcible, illegible, intangible, intelligible, invincible, legible, negligible, producible, reducible**.

In the case of **ible**, there are some words that follow no particular rule, and which you can only try to memorize, such as **collapsible, contemptible, discernible, flexible, gullible**, and **resistible**.

### 7:1e LY, LLY, and ALLY

When forming an adverb from an adjective, the suffix **ly** is added to the word, as in **rich-richly**, or **cruel-cruelly**. If the word already ends in **al**, the ending will be **ally**, as in **actual-actually**.

If the adjective ends in **ic**, the adverb also ends in **ally**, as in **automatically, basically, emphatically, grammatically**, and **systematically**. The only exception to this rule is the word **publicly**.

### 7:1f ANCE and ENCE

If the verb ends in an **r** preceded by a vowel, and is accented on the last syllable, the noun is formed with **ence**: **coherence, conference, deference, inference, preference, reference**.

Otherwise, there is no uniform rule for **ance** and **ence** endings.

### 7:2 100 COMMONLY MISSPELLED WORDS

From the double list of commonly misspelled words that follows, see if you can choose the words that are spelled correctly.

| | A | B |
|---|---|---|
| 1. | absence | abcense |
| 2. | acommodate | accommodate |
| 3. | achievement | achievment |
| 4. | acquiesce | aquiesce |
| 5. | alloted | allotted |
| 6. | analyse | analyze |
| 7. | approximate | aproximate |

| A | B |
|---|---|
| 8. argument | arguement |
| 9. assistent | assistant |
| 10. attendance | attendence |
| 11. banana | bananna |
| 12. begining | beginning |
| 13. believe | beleive |
| 14. changeable | changable |
| 15. collosal | colossal |
| 16. commitment | comitment |
| 17. commitee | committee |
| 18. consede | concede |
| 19. conscientious | consientious |
| 20. consensus | concensus |
| 21. controversy | contreversy |
| 22. criticise | criticize |
| 23. desperate | desparate |
| 24. develope | develop |
| 25. dictionery | dictionary |
| 26. dissapoint | disappoint |
| 27. discriminate | discrimminate |
| 28. drastically | drasticly |
| 29. efficiancy | efficiency |
| 30. eligable | eligible |
| 31. embarrass | embarass |
| 32. exagerate | exaggerate |
| 33. existence | existance |
| 34. forty | fourty |
| 35. friend | freind |
| 36. fullfil | fulfill |
| 37. grammar | grammer |
| 38. imediately | immediately |
| 39. inadvertant | inadvertent |
| 40. infallible | infallable |
| 41. insistent | insistant |
| 42. intersede | intercede |
| 43. interestting | interesting |
| 44. interfered | interferred |
| 45. knowlege | knowledge |
| 46. lisence | license |

| A | B |
|---|---|
| 47. liquefy | liquify |
| 48. loneliness | lonelyness |
| 49. maintanence | maintenance |
| 50. managment | management |
| 51. millionaire | millionnaire |
| 52. morgaged | mortgaged |
| 53. nickle | nickel |
| 54. niece | neice |
| 55. ninty-ninth | ninety-ninth |
| 56. occasionally | ocasionally |
| 57. occurrence | occurence |
| 58. paralyze | paralize |
| 59. permissable | permissible |
| 60. persistant | persistent |
| 61. persuade | pursuade |
| 62. Polaroid | Poleroid |
| 63. preceding | preceeding |
| 64. predictible | predictable |
| 65. preferable | preferible |
| 66. presumptuous | presumtuous |
| 67. privelige | privilege |
| 68. psycological | psychological |
| 69. publicly | publically |
| 70. pursuit | persuit |
| 71. questionaire | questionnaire |
| 72. quizzes | quizes |
| 73. receive | recieve |
| 74. recipiant | recipient |
| 75. reccomend | recommend |
| 76. refered | referred |
| 77. repell | repel |
| 78. repitition | repetition |
| 79. rhythm | rythm |
| 80. safety | safty |
| 81. sieze | seize |
| 82. sincerly | sincerely |
| 83. sincerety | sincerity |
| 84. skillful | skilfull |
| 85. souvenir | souvenier |

|     | A | B |
| --- | --- | --- |
| 86. | specemin | specimen |
| 87. | sueing | suing |
| 88. | superintendant | superintendent |
| 89. | supercede | supersede |
| 90. | suprise | surprise |
| 91. | their | thier |
| 92. | transferable | transferible |
| 93. | truly | truely |
| 94. | unparalleled | unparalelled |
| 95. | usage | useage |
| 96. | vegetible | vegetable |
| 97. | vitious | vicious |
| 98. | Wednesday | Wednsday |
| 99. | weird | wierd |
| 100. | writeing | writing |

(Answers to the spelling quiz are at the end of this chapter.)

## Tips to Correct Answers

1. The six primary spelling rules should have helped you determine the correct spelling of many of the preceding words: words ending in **ible, able**; words ending in **ing, ness,** or **ly**; words beginning with **mis, dis,** or **un.**

2. **ery** and **ary**: Only six common words end in **ery: cemetery, confectionery, distillery, millinery, monastery,** and **stationery** (meaning writing materials). All the rest end in **ary**, such as **secretary.**

3. **ise, ize, yze**: Only two common words end in **yze**, one of them being **analyze.** The majority of the rest end in **ize**, like **authorize, modernize,** or **specialize.** The balance end in **ise,** and you will have to try to remember them. They are the **cise** words, like **exercise**; the **guise** words, like **disguise**; the **mise** words, like **compromise**; the **rise** words, like **sunrise**; the **vise** words, like **advise**; the **wise** words, like **likewise**; and various others, like **advertise** or **merchandise.**

4. **cede, ceed, sede**: Only one word in English ends in **sede,** and that is **supersede.** Only three words end in **ceed**; they are

**exceed**, **proceed**, and **succeed**. The remaining words with this ending are spelled with **cede**, such as **recede**.

5. **efy** and **ify**: A few words, like **stupefy** and **liquefy**, use the **efy** ending. All the rest are spelled with **ify**.

6. **i** before **e**: I comes before **e**, except after **c**, in all words with an **ee** sound, like **believe** and **conceive**. When the word has an **ay** sound, like **beige** and **veil**, the **e** comes first. There are also a few exceptions with the **ee** sound, such as **leisure** and **seize**.

## 7:3 TO HYPHENATE OR NOT

Compound nouns go through a certain progression as they become more commonly used. At first they appear as two words, then as a hyphenated word, and finally as just one word. Good examples of this are the following:

| | | |
|---|---|---|
| book case | book-case | bookcase |
| half back | half-back | halfback |
| rail road | rail-road | railroad |

When in doubt about a compound word, the safest procedure is to consult your dictionary.

### 7:3a Compound Adjectives

Hyphenate an adjective consisting of two or more words when it is followed by a noun.

- She is a good-natured person.
- She is good natured.
- This is the best-known book on the subject.
- This book is the best known.

### 7:3b Suspension Hyphens

When a noun is separated from several modifiers that require the use of a hyphen, the suspension hyphen is used.

- The current rates for first-, second-, and third-class travel are enclosed.
- The new program will have both short- and long-range effects.

## 7:3c Numbers and Fractions

Compound numerals from **twenty-one** through **ninety-nine** use the hyphen. So do fractions like **one-half**.

sixty-seven
one hundred and thirty-eight
three and three-quarters
one-eighth

## 7:3d Three- and Four-Part Compounds

Three- and four-part compounds use the hyphen in most circumstances.

| | |
|---|---|
| free-for-all | jack-in-the-box |
| four-in-hand | jack-of-all-trades |
| hit-and-run (u.m.) | run-of-the-mill (u.m.) |
| son-in-law | mother-in-law |

(**u.m.** means that the expression is hyphenated only when used as a unit modifier, as in a **hit-and-run** driver.)

## 7:3e SELF and HALF

The prefixes **self** and **half** take hyphens.

a self-made man
a half-empty bottle
self-respect
half-truth

## 7:3f Do Not Hyphenate

(1) Do not hyphenate a combination of adverb and adjective.

- He was a highly qualified candidate.
- It is freshly cooked food.

(2) Do not hyphenate a fraction that is used as a noun and followed by **of**.

- The paragraph runs for three quarters of a page.

(3)  Do not use a hyphen between double terms that denote a single office or rank. (This rule is followed by the **New York Times** and the U.S. Government Printing Office, although several other sources may disagree.)

Vice President Smith
Rear Admiral Jones

(4) Prefixes **inter**, **non**, **semi**, and **sub** do not take hyphens unless they are used with proper nouns.

interchange
nonprofit
semiautomatic
substandard
non-Caucasian
non-Christian

## 7:4 CAPITALIZATION GUIDELINES

Everyone knows that the first word of every sentence should be capitalized, as well as the names of people, countries, cities, and streets.

Mr. Andrew Barber
15 Downing Street
London, England

There are a number of other rules for capitalization, however.

### 7:4a Quotations

Capitalize the first word of every direct quotation.

● She said, "Business is improving in all of our branches."

Do not capitalize the first word in an indirect quotation.

● She said that business was improving.

### 7:4b Titles

Titles are capitalized when they refer to specific persons.

the President          Mother
the Senator            Father

Do not capitalize these words if they refer to only one of a class of persons.

- A president has certain specific duties.
- Two senators are elected from each state.

Do not capitalize the names of relatives if they are preceded by possessives.

- My mother is out of town.
- My brother looks very much as Father did at his age.

### 7:4c Deity and Religions

Capitalize names for the Deity, including personal pronouns. Capitalize names for the Bible and other sacred writings, and the names of religions and religious groups. (Again, this rule is followed by the **New York Times** and the U.S. Government Printing Office, although other sources may disagree.)

- God, Jesus Christ, He, Him
- Bible, Koran, Torah, the Scriptures, Book of Genesis
- Protestant, Catholic, Jewish, Shinto, Buddhist

### 7:4d Days and Months

Days and months are capitalized, but the seasons are not.

- Wednesday, Thursday, Friday
- June, July, August
- spring, summer, autumn

### 7:4e Schools and Universities

Names of schools and universities are capitalized, but only when referring to a particular institution.

- Harvard University
- Barnard College
- Evander Childs High School
- She is a high school graduate.
- She attended college in California.

**7:4f** Sections of the Country

Capitalize particular sections of the country, but do not capitalize the points of the compass.

- She lives in the South.
- She drove north to New York City.

**7:4g** Races and Organizations

Capitalize the names of races and organizations.

- Indian, Caucasian, Occidental, Oriental
- League of Women Voters
- National Organization for Women
- National Secretaries Association

**7:4h** Books, Plays, Magazines

The most important words in the titles of books, plays, and magazines should be capitalized.

- **The Last of the Mohicans**
- **Who's Afraid of Virginia Woolf?**
- **The New Yorker**

**7:5** 200 SPECIALIZED BUSINESS WORDS
AND EXPRESSIONS

Every business and profession has special words that are peculiar to itself, such as **arraignment** in law, **fluoroscope** in medicine, or **galley** in publishing. Here are eight groups of such words that you may encounter at some time during your working life.

**7:5a** Accounting

| | | |
|---|---|---|
| accrual | depreciation | ledger |
| auditor | disbursements | liabilities |
| capitalization | fiscal | revenue |
| depletion | | |

**7:5b** Investment and Finance

| | | |
|---|---|---|
| amortization | collateral | portfolio |
| annuity | convertible | pyramiding |
| bearish | debentures | underwriter |
| bill of sale | escrow | yield |
| blue-sky laws | negotiable | |

**7:5c** Insurance

| | | |
|---|---|---|
| actuary | cancellation | liability |
| adjuster | coinsurance | mortality |
| assessment | disability | rider |
| assignment | endowment | salvage |
| beneficiary | floater | subrogation |

**7:5d** Law

| | | |
|---|---|---|
| abatement | eminent domain | notarize |
| actionable | garnishment | statutory law |
| admissible | guaranty | subpoena |
| antitrust | indemnification | suretyship |
| arraignment | injunction | testimonium clause |
| attestation | interstate commerce | tort |
| bailment | intrastate commerce | usury |
| bankruptcy | legal tender | waiver |
| codicil | negotiable instrument | warranty |
| decedent | nonnegotiable instrument | writ |

**7:5e** Medicine

| | | |
|---|---|---|
| abscess | diabetes | pneumonia |
| acupuncture | diathermy | prognosis |
| adrenal | electrocardiogram | prophylaxis |
| alimentary | emollient | psoriasis |
| antibiotic | fibrillation | psychiatrist |
| bacteriology | fluoroscope | psychosomatic |
| barbiturate | hemoglobin | purgative |
| cardiograph | hemorrhage | surgeon |
| cathartic | neurology | therapy |
| catheter | pituitary | |
| cerebral | placebo | |

## 7:5f Publishing

| | | |
|---|---|---|
| agate | format | logo |
| appendix | galley | lowercase |
| artwork | gravure | microfiche |
| bibliography | halftone | mimeograph |
| boldface | hectograph | monotype |
| byline | informatics | offset |
| copyfitting | italic | repagination |
| copyright | letterpress | typography |
| cropping | lightface | uppercase |
| databank | line cut | videodisk |
| dummy | linotype | viewdata |
| electrotype | lithograph | widow |

## 7:5g Real Estate

| | | |
|---|---|---|
| amortization | grantee | quitclaim deed |
| appurtenances | grantor | right-of-way |
| attestation | leasehold | sale-and-leaseback |
| chattel mortgage | lessee | testimonium clause |
| conveyance | lessor | vendee |
| easement | lien | vendor |
| equity | marketable title | warranty deed |
| floor/area ratio | mortgagee | zoning |
| foreclosure | mortgagor | |

## 7:5h Television and Radio

| | | |
|---|---|---|
| actualities | hot switch | reception |
| anchor person | intercutting | satellite |
| bird feed | master shot | short-form series |
| bite | mini-camera | sit-com |
| closed-caption | newscaster | telecast |
| close-up | newscenter | Telstar |
| commentator | one-shot | transmission |
| coverage | pilot | voice over |
| cue card | prime time (noun) | voice wrap |
| dee-jay | prime-time (adj.) | whiparound |
| documentary | pubcaster | |
| ee-jay | rebroadcast | |

Answers to Spelling Test

| | | | | |
|---|---|---|---|---|
| 1. A | 21. A | 41. A | 61. A | 81. B |
| 2. B | 22. B | 42. B | 62. A | 82. B |
| 3. A | 23. A | 43. B | 63. A | 83. B |
| 4. A | 24. B | 44. A | 64. B | 84. A |
| 5. B | 25. B | 45. B | 65. A | 85. A |
| 6. B | 26. B | 46. B | 66. A | 86. B |
| 7. A | 27. A | 47. A | 67. B | 87. B |
| 8. A | 28. A | 48. A | 68. B | 88. B |
| 9. B | 29. B | 49. B | 69. A | 89. B |
| 10. A | 30. B | 50. B | 70. A | 90. B |
| 11. A | 31. A | 51. B | 71. B | 91. A |
| 12. B | 32. B | 52. B | 72. A | 92. A |
| 13. A | 33. A | 53. B | 73. A | 93. A |
| 14. A | 34. A | 54. A | 74. B | 94. A |
| 15. B | 35. A | 55. B | 75. B | 95. A |
| 16. A | 36. B | 56. A | 76. B | 96. B |
| 17. B | 37. A | 57. A | 77. B | 97. B |
| 18. B | 38. B | 58. A | 78. B | 98. A |
| 19. A | 39. B | 59. B | 79. A | 99. A |
| 20. A | 40. A | 60. B | 80. A | 100. B |

CONCLUSION

One misspelled word can spoil the effect of an entire letter. When in doubt, consult your dictionary.

# 8. BASIC LETTER WRITING TECHNIQUES

You can greatly increase your value as a secretary with the ability to compose simple business letters, memos, and reports. The letters you write should be attractive and easy to understand. Keep this in mind, whether you type letters yourself or dictate them for transcription by someone else.

## 8:1 PARAGRAPH DIVISION MADE SIMPLE

A letter is always appealing when it is divided into fairly short paragraphs, composed of sentences no more than twenty words in length.

### 8:1a The Short Letter

Note how much easier it is to read the following letter when it is divided into shorter paragraphs instead of one forbidding block.

Dear Mr. Perrin:

We sincerely regret the unsatisfactory service you received from one of our repairmen recently. As a regular customer, you should know that such service is not customary. We carefully select and supervise our employees to make sure that our customers are taken care of efficiently and courteously. When this is not the case, we appreciate having the matter called to our attention. Thank you for taking the time to write to us. We shall try even harder in the future to give you the kind of service you expect.

Cordially,

In this second version of the same letter, you will note that the main subject is contained in the middle paragraph while the opening and closing thoughts appear in separate paragraphs, with a more easily readable effect.

Dear Mr. Perrin:

We sincerely regret the unsatisfactory service you received from one of our repairmen recently.

As a regular customer, you should know that such service is not customary. We carefully select and supervise our employees to make sure that our customers are taken care of efficiently and courteously. When this is not the case, we appreciate having the matter called to our attention.

Thank you for taking the time to write to us. We shall try even harder in the future to give you the kind of service you expect.

Cordially,

**8:1b** The Long Letter

In a longer letter the paragraphing becomes a bit more complicated, but there is only one rule to remember. Each paragraph should cover a single subject or a specific part of a larger topic. In other words, every time the thought changes a new paragraph is required. Try to apply this idea in the following letter.

Dear Mrs. Quincy:

Everyone these days is looking for ways to beat inflation. One of the most effective methods is to order in volume whenever possible to take advantage of quantity discounts. Our records show that during the past year you purchased 200 carbon motor brushes. Since you never ordered more than thirty of these at a single time, you bought at a higher price than necessary, as discounts apply only on purchases of fifty or more. In amounts of fifty for each order you could have cut your total costs for the year by ten percent. That would have meant considerable savings for you and, if you had ordered in quantities of 100, you could have saved another eight percent. We are always ready to cooperate with customers, like yourself, who have good credit, so why not discuss it with one of our representatives? We hope to hear from you soon.

Cordially,

Into how many paragraphs would you divide the preceding letter? Five is the correct answer.

The first paragraph gives a general idea of the subject of the letter. The second provides details concerning this particular customer's purchases for the previous year, and the third presents a purchase plan that would save the customer money. The fourth paragraph suggests that the customer take action, and the final paragraph expresses the hope for an early reply. (See the end of this chapter for the corrected letter.)

## 8:2 KEEPING STATEMENTS POSITIVE

Almost any statement can be written in either a negative or a positive way. Some people unconsciously fall into the habit of stating things negatively. This is a habit that must be corrected if one is to write effective letters. Notice how much stronger the following sentences are when they are expressed in a positive way.

(1)
**Negative**

- If you will send us your credit card number and expiration date, we will try to fill your order.

**Positive**

- Please send us your credit card number and expiration date, and your order will be filled promptly.

(2)
**Negative**

- I believe you will find our service to be valuable.

**Positive**

● I know you will find our service to be valuable.

(3)
**Negative**

● We cannot make delivery on the date you mention.

**Positive**

● We will make delivery as close to the desired date as possible.

(4)
**Negative**

● We have very few dissatisfied clients.

**Positive**

● We have many satisfied clients.

In example 1, there are two weak words, **if** and **try**, in the negative statement. These have been eliminated in the positive version. In example 2, the weak word **believe** has been replaced by the stronger **know**. In example 3, the weak phrase **We cannot** has been replaced by the stronger **We will**. In example 4, the negative word **dissatisfied** has been replaced by the positive word **satisfied**.

Certain words automatically produce a negative reaction in the reader of a letter. These words include **think, hope, may, might, refuse, delay,** and **impossible.** Words such as **pleasure, convenience, promptly, service, happy, satisfactory,** and **appreciate** induce a more favorable reaction.

**8:2a** 265 Positive Words

| | | | |
|---|---|---|---|
| able | assert | brilliant | confident |
| absolutely | assist | broad | congratulate |
| accommodate | assure | candid | cooperate |
| advantage | bargain | capable | courtesy |
| agree | basic | certain | declare |
| alleviate | beautiful | clear | dedicate |
| amicable | benefit | compatible | definite |
| anticipate | boundless | concur | demonstrate |

| | | | |
|---|---|---|---|
| dependable | friendly | legitimate | natural |
| desire | fulfill | liberate | necessary |
| determine | future | liberty | negotiate |
| develop | gainful | lifelong | numerous |
| direct | genuine | like | nurture |
| distinct | gigantic | live | nutrient |
| eager | glamour | lively | objective |
| easy | glorious | longevity | oblige |
| efficient | goal | love | obtain |
| elated | grateful | lovely | offer |
| enable | great | lucky | often |
| encourage | growth | lucrative | onward |
| endeavor | handle | lustrous | opportune |
| enhance | happy | luxury | opportunity |
| enrich | helpful | magical | optimism |
| enthusiasm | high | magnetic | orderly |
| establish | idea | magnificent | original |
| excellent | ideal | magnitude | palatable |
| exciting | immense | majesty | palatial |
| expedite | impel | major | particular |
| explore | impetus | manageable | payment |
| express | implement | manifest | peaceful |
| extraordinary | important | markedly | perfect |
| facilitate | improve | marvel | perfectly |
| favor | incentive | marvelous | permanent |
| feasible | increase | massive | perpetual |
| fervent | indelible | masterful | persevere |
| fine | indomitable | matchless | persistence |
| first | infallible | mellow | personality |
| flair | infinite | merit | pertinent |
| fluent | influence | mettle | pervading |
| formative | ingenious | might | pleasant |
| formulate | inimitable | miracle | please |
| fortify | integrity | modern | pleasure |
| fortitude | intense | momentous | plentiful |
| fortunate | invaluable | motivation | plus |
| foundation | invincible | moving | popular |
| free | jubilant | multiply | positive |
| freedom | kind | munificent | prestige |
| fresh | lasting | mutual | produce |

| | | | |
|---|---|---|---|
| productive | salutary | standard | terrific |
| proficient | sanction | steady | thank |
| propitious | sane | strength | therapy |
| quick | satisfaction | stupendous | thorough |
| quickly | satisfactory | substantiate | timely |
| reasonable | satisfy | subtle | together |
| recommend | scientific | success | total |
| regular | secure | successful | tranquil |
| respect | security | superb | transform |
| responsible | shield | superior | tremendous |
| restful | significant | superlative | trustworthy |
| revenue | smooth | support | uncommon |
| revitalize | solid | supreme | undoubtedly |
| revive | soothing | surely | unforgettable |
| reward | sparkling | surmount | unique |
| safe | special | surpass | unlimited |
| safety | spectacular | sustaining | |
| salient | splendid | sympathy | |
| salubrious | spontaneous | tenacious | |

## 8:3 THE TRICK OF THE FIVE W's

Newspaper reporters have one inflexible writing rule, known as **the five W's**. The five W's that every reporter must remember are **who**, **what**, **when**, **where**, and **why**. The writer of a business letter should be equally concrete and specific. Like the reporter, you want to convey the clearest and most complete message in the fewest possible words.

**Vague**

Dear Sir:

Our sales manager is away from the office and is not expected back for some time.

Meanwhile, I want to assure you that your order is being taken care of, and will be shipped to you at the earliest possible date.

Your patronage is appreciated, and we are more than happy to be of service.

Sincerely,

## Specific

Dear Mr. Roberts:

John Orwell (**who**), our sales manager, is away (**why**), on vacation (**where**) and is not expected back until July 5 (**when**).

Meanwhile, I want to assure you that your order of June 15 (**when**), for three portable electric typewriters (**what**), will be shipped to you within the week (**when**).

Your patronage is appreciated, and we at Chickering Company (**who**) are more than happy to be of service.

Sincerely,

You will note that the specific letter not only deals in concrete facts, names, and dates, but it also sounds more personal. Your company and their clients are not abstractions, but groups of human beings, and you should write a business letter as one person to another, with all the consideration that entails.

## **8:4** ELIMINATION OF NEEDLESS WORDS

Besides being concrete and specific, the good business letter is simple and direct. Your writing, like your speech, should be free of useless, empty words. In the letter that follows the unnecessary words are underlined. Notice how much better it reads without them.

Dear Mr. Carruthers:

Due to the fact that we have recently expanded our operations, we are now in need of new steel shelving. We would like something along the lines of the shelving we purchased from you in the year of 1982, for the purpose of storing office supplies.

In the event that you still have this shelving in stock, please send us your catalog and price list in order that we may make a selection.

Thanking you in advance,

Sincerely,

Dear Mr. Carruthers:

Since we have recently expanded our operation, we now need new steel shelving. We would like something similar to the shelving we purchased from you in 1982, for storing office supplies.

If you still have this shelving in stock, please send us your catalog and price list so that we may make a selection.

Thank you very much.

Sincerely,

## 8:4a Business Clichés

Some unnecessary phrases have become so commonplace in business letters that we use them automatically, without thinking. Stop and think next time.

| Cliché | Preferable |
| --- | --- |
| We take the liberty | We are |
| Attached hereto | Attached is |
| Enclosed herewith | Enclosed is |
| Enclosed please find | Enclosed is |
| Hoping for the favor of a reply | Look forward to hearing from you |
| We wish to acknowledge receipt | We have received |
| Kindly advise | Please let us know |
| Your letter of recent date | Your recent letter |
| We have not been favored with an answer | We have not received your answer |
| We beg to inform you | You will be interested to learn |
| Thanking you for your kind attention | We shall appreciate your attention |

The following should also be avoided:

| | |
| --- | --- |
| would advise | contents noted |
| and oblige | under separate cover |
| pending receipt | wish to state |

## 8:5 SIMPLE GUIDE TO EFFECTIVE LETTERS

The most effective letter is one that emphasizes the recipient's point of view. When possible, avoid the overuse of I and **we**, especially at the beginning of a sentence.

### 8:5a The You Emphasis

Sentences beginning with I or **We**, can often be restated to begin with **You**.

| I-We Emphasis | You Emphasis |
| --- | --- |
| We are pleased to inform you ... | You will be pleased to learn ... |
| I would like you to attend ... | You will no doubt want to attend ... |
| We follow this procedure because ... | You will benefit from this procedure because ... |
| We raised $50,000 last year. | You and other contributors donated $50,000 last year. |

### 8:5b Good Correspondence Manners

Be as polite to your correspondents as you would be if you were face to face with them. Remember to say "please," "thank you," and "I am sorry."

**Poor Manners**

Dear Mrs. Davies:

We have your letter in which you claim that the cosmetic kit you purchased has not proved satisfactory. You are the first customer to register such a complaint, and we are at a loss to understand it.

We will, however, pick up the package by UPS so that it can be returned to us, if you will let us know the time and day that will be convenient. Also, will you inform us whether you wish to receive a replacement, a credit, or a cash refund?

We are sorry if you were inconvenienced.

Sincerely,

### Good Manners

Dear Mrs. Davies:

Your letter arrived this morning, and we are very sorry to learn that the cosmetic kit you purchased has not proved satisfactory. We want our customers to be happy with our merchandise, and we thank you for bringing the matter to our attention.

Will you kindly let us know the time and day when it will be convenient to have this package picked up by UPS and returned? Also, will you inform us whether you wish to receive a replacement, a credit, or a cash refund?

We regret the inconvenience that was caused you, and we hope to continue to serve you in the future.

Cordially,

A few simple changes in wording can transform a discourteous letter into a courteous one.

| Poor Manners | Good Manners |
|---|---|
| You claim you did not receive the merchandise we sent you. | We are sorry to learn that you did not receive the merchandise you ordered. |
| We request that you send us ... | Please send us ... |
| We have received your order. | Thank you for your order. |
| You must have been misinformed. | Evidently you did not know ... |
| You failed to send ... | We have not received ... |
| We regret that we must refuse ... | We regret that we are unable ... |

### 8:5c Clarity of Meaning

The best business letters are clear and concise. Try to avoid ambiguous language that is subject to more than one interpretation.

| Unclear | Clear |
|---|---|
| We sell at a discount **only** in our annex. | We sell at a discount in our annex **only**. |

| **Unclear** | **Clear** |
|---|---|
| We will return the contracts that we received in error **by registered mail.** | We will return **by registered mail** the contracts that we received in error. |
| The Farrar Brothers have always supplied newsdealers with paperback books and magazines, but **they** still do not accept as many returns as **they** would like **them** to. | The Farrar Brothers have always supplied newsdealers with paperback books and magazines, but the **Farrar Brothers** do not accept as many returns as **the newsdealers** would like **them** to. |

## 8:5d Openings and Closings

The opening paragraph of any letter should be phrased in such a way that it immediately captures the reader's interest. Depending on the type of letter, the closing paragraph should spur the reader to action or leave the reader with a feeling of reassurance.

(1) **Openings**: Here are a few sample openings, with examples of how they can be improved.

| | |
|---|---|
| **Dull** | We wish to acknowledge receipt of your letter of July 5. |
| **Improved** | We appreciate your letter of July 5. |
| **Dull** | We have your letter of May 2. |
| **Improved** | We regret to learn from your letter of May 2 ... We are happy to learn from your letter of May 2 ... |
| **Dull** | Thank you for your order. |
| **Improved** | Thank you for your order for six copies of Faulkner's **Sanctuary.** |
| **Dull** | We regret that we cannot comply with your request. |
| **Improved** | We have given careful consideration to your request. |
| **Dull** | Replying to your request ... |
| **Improved** | Thank you very much for your inquiry of December 1. |

| | |
|---|---|
| **Dull** | Replying to yours of the twelfth ... |
| **Improved** | Thank you for the opportunity to answer your inquiry of November 12. |

(2) **Closings:** Here are a few sample closings, with examples of how they can be improved.

| | |
|---|---|
| **Dull** | Hoping to hear from you soon ... |
| **Improved** | We will be glad to hear from you. |
| **Dull** | Looking forward to your reply ... |
| **Improved** | We look forward to hearing from you. |
| **Dull** | We enclose a form for your convenience. |
| **Improved** | Please sign and mail the enclosed form. |
| **Dull** | We shall appreciate prompt payment. |
| **Improved** | We shall appreciate your check for $350 by return mail. |
| **Dull** | Thanking you, we are ... |
| **Improved** | Thank you for your interest. |
| | Thank you for your assistance. |
| | Thank you for your order. |
| **Dull** | We trust we have been of assistance. |
| **Improved** | Please let us know if we can be of further assistance. |
| **Dull** | We look forward to hearing from you. |
| **Improved** | We look forward to the opportunity of serving you. |
| **Dull** | That is all the information I can give you. |
| **Improved** | I hope this information has been helpful to you. |
| **Dull** | Thank you for writing. |
| **Improved** | Do not hesitate to write us at any time. |

## 8:6 SEXIST LANGUAGE AND HOW TO AVOID IT

Many sex-related expressions which were perfectly acceptable a few years ago now seem old-fashioned and offensive. It is condescending to refer to grown women as **girls**. Never call a person's secretary a **girl**. If your own executive refers to a secretary that way, you should tactfully call the error to his or her attention.

## 8:6a MAN, WOMAN, or PERSON

The prefix or suffix **man** poses problems that can be overcome with a little ingenuity. You can use the word **manpower** to refer to men available for a certain task, or **womanpower** to refer to women available for some purpose. When you are referring to a mixed group, it sounds silly to call it **peoplepower** or **personpower**. A wiser choice would be some other expression, such as **work force**.

| male | female | male and female |
|------|--------|-----------------|
| manpower | womanpower | work force |

**Man** or **mankind** can be expressed better as **the human race**, when that is the intended meaning. **Man** as a verb, in an expression like "**man** the machines," is inappropriate if some of the operators are women. Say "the workers are **operating** the machines," rather than "the workers are **manning** the machines."

| male | female | male and female |
|------|--------|-----------------|
| mankind | womankind | the human race |
| man (verb) | operate | operate |

**Manslaughter**, meaning the unintentional taking of human life, is a legal term and should not be changed.

When **man** is used as a suffix, as in **chairman**, **layman**, or **workman**, you may want to find substitutes for referring to women or to persons of either sex. **Lay person** sounds fine and is usable. **Workperson** sounds silly and should be changed to **worker**. **Chairperson** and **chairwoman** are sometimes used, but **The New York Times** still uses the conventional **chairman** when describing a female company official. The male or female conductor of a meeting may simply be referred to as **the chair**.

| male | female | male and/or female |
|------|--------|--------------------|
| businessman | businesswoman | businessperson or businesspersons (businesspeople) |
| chairman | chairman (company official) chairperson chairwoman | the chair (meeting conductor) |

| male | female | male and/or female |
|------|--------|--------------------|
| congressman | congresswoman | member of Congress |
| layman | lay person | lay person or persons |
| policeman | policewoman | police officer or officers |
| salesman | saleswoman | salesperson or salespersons (salespeople) |
| workman | worker | worker or workers |

**8:6b** ESS or TRIX

The **ess** ending, to indicate femininity, is acceptable in the word **actress**. **Heiress** is another word that is difficult to change without losing the precise meaning, and **heirs** can be used to indicate a mixed group. It is patronizing, however, to refer to a woman poet as a **poetess**, or to a woman author as an **authoress**. A **hostess** can be referred to as a **host** or **hostess**, and a **host** and **hostess** can be called **the hosts**.

| male | female | male and female |
|------|--------|-----------------|
| actor | actress | actors |
| author | author | authors |
| heir | heiress | heirs |
| host | host, hostess | hosts |
| poet | poet | poets |

The **trix** ending is acceptable in the legal term **executrix**, but the word **aviatrix** is extremely dated. Either **aviator or pilot** is preferable.

| male | female | male and female |
|------|--------|-----------------|
| aviator | aviator | aviators |
| executor | executrix | executors |

**8:6c** MRS., MISS, or MS.

In business, the title **Ms.** has become an all-purpose title when you do not know whether to address a woman as **Mrs.** or **Miss**.

While some feminists prefer to be addressed as **Ms.**, the use of **Mrs.** or **Miss** is usually preferable when you know which title is appropriate. A recent national poll shows that 77 percent of all American women do not like the title **Ms.**, and would prefer **Miss** or **Mrs.**

Sometimes the title is dropped altogether, and a woman is saluted as "Dear Mary Jones:" but I would recommend this usage only on occasions when you feel very sure that the person addressed will not take offense at the apparent familiarity.

If a woman signs her letters "Ethel Farragut (Guggenheim)," you can address her either as "**Miss** Farragut" or **Mrs.** Guggenheim." When the signature gives no indication of marital status, then **Ms.** or **Miss** can be used, although **Miss** is preferable. A woman who wants to be called **Mrs.** should put **Mrs.** in parentheses after her signature.

In signing your own letters, it shows consideration for your correspondents to indicate how you wish to be addressed by adding **(Mrs.)**, **(Miss)**, or **(Ms.)** after your signature.

## 8:6d HIS, HER, and THEIR

We have dealt with this problem in Chapter 5 under **Correct Choice of Gender**. The pronoun **his** can no longer be used to refer to either sex, as in "Every employee is expected to perform **his** duties to the best of **his** ability." The simplest way to handle this is to write the sentence in the plural.

- All employees are expected to perform **their** duties to the best of **their** ability.

Otherwise, you have to use **his or her** or **his/her** versions, which can be awkward. You cannot combine a singular subject with a plural pronoun, however, without being grammatically incorrect.

| **Never say:** | **Each** employee is entitled to **their** own locker. |
| **You must say:** | **Each** employee is entitled to **his or her** own locker. |

Answer to 8:1b, The Long Letter

Dear Mrs. Quincy:

Everyone these days is looking for ways to beat inflation. One of the most effective methods is to order in volume whenever possible to take advantage of quantity discounts.

Our records show that during the past year you purchased 200 carbon motor brushes. Since you never ordered more than thirty of these at a single time, you bought at a higher price than necessary, as discounts apply only on purchases of fifty or more.

In amounts of fifty for each order you could have cut your total costs for the year by ten percent. That would have meant considerable savings for you and, if you had ordered in quantities of 100, you could have saved another eight percent.

We are always ready to cooperate with customers, like yourself, who have good credit, so why not discuss it with one of our representatives?

We hope to hear from you soon.

Sincerely,

## CONCLUSION

Write the sort of letter that you would like to receive yourself—cordial, informative, and easy to understand.

## CHART III: SPELLING TIPS

Many spelling rules, as you know, have their exceptions, but here are some tips that will help you.

**1.** Doubling Final Consonants

When the final consonant is preceded by a single vowel and the suffix begins with a vowel, the consonant is doubled. This is true for one-syllable words like **plan** or **run** (**planning**, **running**), and for multi-syllable words that are accented on the last syllable, like **begin** or **control** (**beginner**, **controller**).

**2.** Dropping the Silent E

A final silent **e** is usually dropped before a suffix beginning with a vowel (**exciting**, **movable**), but the **e** is retained before a suffix beginning with a consonant (**excitement**, **movement**).

**3.** MIS, DIS, and UN

These prefixes all follow the same forumla. They do not become **miss**, **diss**, or **unn** unless the root word begins with **s** or **n**.

**misshapen**
**dissatisfy**
**unnatural**

**4.** I Before E

The old rhyme, "I before **e** except after **c**," holds true in all words with the **ee** sound, except **leisure** and **seize**.

## CHART IV: THREE HANDY RULES OF GRAMMAR

Rule #1: WAS/WERE, IS/ARE, WE/US, I/ME

Make your choice by isolating unnecessary words and cutting the sentence down to the bare essentials.

- The **letter** (with its enclosures) **was** mailed yesterday.
- **Each** (of you) **is** expected to cooperate.
- Some of **us** (women) were promoted.
- **We** (women) want equal rights.
- The memorandum was for (Miss Grimes and) **me**.

Rule #2: HE/HIM, SHE/HER

Reverse the sentence structure to make the correct answer apparent.

- It was **he/him**.
  **He** was it.
  It was **he**.
- The first to appear were **she/her** and Mr. Forbes.
  **She** and Mr. Forbes were the first to appear.
  The first to appear were **she** and Mr. Forbes.

Rule #3: WHO/WHOM

The **who/whom** choice can be made in several ways.
a. **Cutting**

- **Who** (shall I say) is calling?

b. **Reversal**

- **Who/whom** do you wish to speak with?
  With **whom** do you wish to speak?
  **Whom** do you wish to speak with?

c. **Reversal plus substitution of he/she or him/her.**

- **Who/whom** do you wish to assist you?
  Do you wish **her** (**whom**) to assist you?
  **Whom** do you wish to assist you?

# Part 3

# ATTRACTIVE LETTERS

# 9. FORMS OF ADDRESS

Most business correspondence is addressed to private individuals or corporations, and the forms of address are familiar to the average secretary. Occasions do arise, however, when you must address an official of some sort, and you do not want to make a blunder. This chapter will deal with such specialized problems, and many other questions related to correct modes of address.

## 9:1 BUSINESS ADDRESS

A company, corporation, federation, league, or association is always addressed as **Gentlemen**. This may be subject to change, since many women are now involved in business management, but it is advisable to use traditional salutation at present.

Thomas Aiken Company, Inc.
234 Fourth Avenue
New York, New York 10003
Gentlemen:

In addressing a French company, the word **Messieurs** takes the place of **Gentlemen**.

Galleries Lafayette
Rue de la Paix
Paris, France
Messieurs:

An organization composed principally of women is, of course, addressed as **Ladies**.

League of Women Voters
817 Broadway
New York, New York 10003

Ladies:

When the membership of an organization is obviously composed of both sexes, then the proper address is **Ladies and Gentlemen**.

American Federation of Teachers
1012 14 Street N.W.
Washington, D.C. 20005

Ladies and Gentlemen:


**9:1a** Male Address

A company official's title is not used in the salutation of the letter.

Mr. William Granville, President
H.L. Mencken Corporation
(local address)

Dear Mr. Granville:

When a letter is addressed to the attention of an individual in a corporation, the proper salutation is **Gentlemen**.

Texas Oil Corporation
(local address)
                                    Attention Mr. Harry Hansen

Gentlemen:

Two individual men addressed simultaneously are addressed in succession by full name, and the higher ranking man is mentioned first. Otherwise, they are listed alphabetically.

Mr. Robert Haines and
Mr. Stuart James
(local address)

Dear Mr. Haines and Mr. James:

**9:1 b** Female Address

A married businesswoman is addressed by her own first name rather than her husband's, as she would be in social life. She is called **Mrs.** unless she prefers **Miss** or **Ms.**

Mrs. Elizabeth Manderville
Sears and Ward Company
(local address)

Dear Mrs. Manderville:

Outside of business, a married woman is addressed by **Mrs.** followed by her husband's name. Widows are addressed similarly.

Mrs. John Manderville
(local address)

Dear Mrs. Manderville:

A divorcée should be addressed as **Mrs.** followed by her maiden name and former husband's surname, unless she prefers to use her own first name, or even revert completely to her maiden name.

Mrs. Smith Jones
(local address)

Dear Mrs. Jones:

Mrs. Sally Jones
(local address)

Dear Mrs. Jones:

Miss Sally Smith
(local Address)

Dear Miss Smith:

A single woman should be addressed as **Miss**, unless she indicates a preference for **Ms.**

Miss Paula Pringle
Rubin and Stern Company
(local address)

Dear Miss Pringle:

Two women should be addressed in succession by full name. If one is of higher rank than the other, her name should be mentioned first.

Mrs. Theresa Thompson and
Miss Ursula Williams
(local Address)
Dear Mrs. Thompson and Miss Williams:
**or**
Ladies:

When a man and a woman are addressed simultaneously, the woman's name is always mentioned first.

Miss Ursula Williams and
Mr. Arnold Baker
(local address)
Dear Miss Williams and Mr. Baker:

If you do not know a woman's marital status, it is best to address her as **Miss**, and allow her to correct you later if necessary.

When your correspondent's first name can belong to either a man or a woman, you should inquire for the correct information, rather than risk a mistake.

As a last resort, you can address someone as "Dear Dana Smith" when either sex or marital status are in question, but this usage should not become regular practice.

When a letter is addressed to the attention of an individual woman in a corporation, the proper salutation is still **Gentlemen** unless you know that many of the corporation's officials are of both sexes, in which case **Ladies and Gentlemen** would be appropriate:

The Simmons Construction Company
(local address)
                            Attention: Miss Sarah Collins
Gentlemen:

Taylor Designs, Inc.
(local address)
                            Attention: Mrs. Carol Kayne
Ladies and Gentlemen:

If the organization being addressed is a wholly female one, naturally the salutation would be **Ladies**.

National Organization for Women
(local address)
                    Attention: Miss Norma Owens
    Ladies:

## 9:1c Doctors and Lawyers

When the signature on a letter is followed by the initials of a doctorate, that means the writer expects to be addressed as **Dr.**

Katherine Karlin, Ph.D.
(local address)
Dear Dr. Karlin:

Lawrence Langer, M.D.
(local address)
Dear Dr. Langer:

Martin Manville, D.D.S.
(local address)
Dear Dr. Manville:

Norma Mailor, D.V.M.
(local address)
Dear Dr. Mailor:

You can address a doctor as **Dr. Lawrence Langer**, without the initials, but do not use titles on both ends of a name. **Never** write **Dr. Lawrence Langer, M.D.**

A doctor and his wife are addressed as **Dr. and Mrs.**

Dr. and Mrs. Lawrence Langer
(local address)
Dear Dr. and Mrs. Langer:

A woman doctor and her husband would be addressed as **Dr. and Mr.**

Dr. Lillian Langer and Mr. Lawrence Langer
(local address)

Dear Dr. and Mr. Langer:

Lawyers' titles are mentioned in the address, beneath their names, but they are saluted the same as lay persons.

Bailey, Cranshaw, and Daniels
Attorneys at Law
(local address)

Gentlemen:

Mr. David Erikson
Attorney at Law
(local address)

Dear Mr. Erikson:

Mrs. Carol Framish
Attorney at Law
(local address)

Dear Mrs. Framish:

## 9:2 GOVERNMENT OFFICIALS

**Honorable** is an all-purpose title, applicable to most state, local, or federal government officials; but certain personages, like the President, are not addressed that way until they are out of office.

The President and Vice President are never addressed by name.

The President
The White House
Washington, D.C. 20500

Dear Mr. President:

The Vice President
Dirksen Senate Office Building
Washington, D.C. 20510

Dear Mr. Vice President:

A former President is known as **Honorable**, unless he also has a military title. He is saluted as **Mr.**

Honorable Chester Alan Arthur
(local address)

Dear Mr. Arthur:

## 9:2a State and Local

The traditional way of addressing governors and mayors is **Honorable**, but you can address a governor or mayor simply as **Governor** or **Mayor** if you like.

### 1. Governors

Honorable Frank Knight
Governor of Colorado
Executive Chambers
Denver, Colorado 80202

Dear Governor Knight:

Governor Frank Knight
Executive Chambers
Denver, Colorado 80202

Dear Governor Knight:

The governor of Massachusetts is known as **His** or **Her Excellency**.

His Excellency, the Governor of Massachusetts
State House
Boston, Massachusetts 02109

Dear Sir:

Acting governors may be addressed as **Honorable**, but they are saluted as **Mr.**, **Mrs.**, or **Miss**.

Honorable Albert Leonard
Acting Governor of Nevada
Executive Chambers
Carson City, Nevada 89701

Dear Mr. Leonard:

Lieutenant governors are saluted by title, or as **Mr., Mrs.,** or **Miss**.

Honorable Grace C. Mathews
Lieutenant Governor of Kentucky
Senate Chamber
Frankfort, Kentucky 40601

Dear Lt. Governor Mathews (or Dear Mrs. Mathews):

When you do not know a governor's name, address him or her as **The Honorable** plus title. The governor is then saluted as **Dear Sir, Dear Madam,** or by title.

The Honorable Governor of Oregon
Executive Chambers
Salem, Oregon 97301

Dear Sir (or Dear Mr. Governor)


## 2. Other State Officials

The state attorney general and secretary of state are entitled to an **Honorable** and they are saluted by their official titles.

Honorable Clifford M. Nolan
Attorney General of Texas
State Capitol
Austin, Texas 78710

Dear Attorney General Nolan (or Dear Mr. Attorney General):

Honorable David Ottinger
Secretary of State of Texas
State Capitol
Austin, Texas 78710

Dear Secretary Ottinger (or Dear Mr. Secretary):

All state senators, including the president of the senate, are called **Dear Senator** or **Dear Mr., Mrs.,** or **Miss**.

Honorable Joseph Palling
President of the Senate of the State of New York
Albany, New York 12224

Dear Senator Palling:

Senator Norman Quigley
New York State Senate
Albany, New York 12224

Dear Mr. Quigley:

All members of the assembly are called **Dear Assemblyman** or **Dear Assemblywoman**. Representatives or delegates are addressed as **Honorable** and are called **Mr.**, **Mrs.**, or **Miss**.

Honorable Paul Rowland
Speaker of the Assembly of the State of New York
Albany, New York 12224

Dear Assemblyman Rowland:

Assemblywoman Ruth Stevens
Legislative Office Building
Albany, New York 12224

Dear Assemblywoman Stevens:

Honorable Max Steuben
House of Representatives
Montgomery, Alabama 36104

Dear Mr. Steuben:

The state treasurer, auditor, or comptroller is also entitled to **Honorable** and is addressed by the name of the office or as **Mr.**, **Mrs.**, or **Miss**.

Honorable Oscar Thompson
Comptroller of the State of California
State Office Building
Sacramento, California 95813

Dear Comptroller Thompson (or Dear Mr. Thompson):

### 3. Local Officials

The mayor of a city is addressed as **Honorable** or **Mayor** and is saluted as **Mayor**.

Honorable Herbert Vielehr
Mayor of the City of New York
City Hall
New York, New York 10007

Dear Mayor Vielehr:

Mayor Herbert Vielehr
City Hall
New York, New York 10007

Dear Mayor Vielehr:

The president of the Board of Commissioners is addressed and saluted as **Mr.**, **Mrs.**, or **Miss**, or is given the title of **Honorable** and addressed as **President**.

Mr. Isaac Wilder, President
Board of Commissioners of the City of New York
City Hall
New York, New York 10007

Dear Mr. Wilder:

Honorable Isaac Wilder, President
Board of Commissioners of the City of New York
City Hall
New York, New York 10007

Dear President Wilder:

An alderman is addressed as **Alderman** and saluted as **Mr.**, **Mrs.**, or **Miss**.

Alderman Brian Wilcox
City Hall
Minneapolis, Minnesota 55401

Dear Mr. Wilcox:

A city council member is addressed and saluted as **Councilman** or **Councilwoman**, but can also be addressed as **Honorable** and saluted as **Mr.**, **Mrs.**, or **Miss**.

Councilman James Yates
City Council
City Hall
New York, New York 10007

Dear Councilman Yates:

Honorable Jane Yates
City Council
City Hall
New York, New York 10007

Dear Miss Yates:

**9:2b** Federal

The President is always addressed as **The President** and **Dear Mr. President**, even when he and his wife are addressed jointly.

The President and Mrs. Adams
The White House
Washington, D.C. 20500
Dear Mr. President and Mrs. Adams:

If the President were a woman, she would be addressed as **The President** and **Dear Madam President**, even when she and her husband were addressed jointly.

The President and Mr. Adams
The White House
Washington, D.C. 20500
Dear Madam President and Mr. Adams:

Presidential secretaries are called **Honorable**, with the exception of the Press Secretary and secretaries who retain military rank.

Honorable Lyle Cantor
Secretary to the President
The White House
Washington, D.C. 20500
Dear Mr. Cantor:

Honorable Mabel Dodge
Assistant Secretary to the President
The White House
Washington, D.C . 20500
Dear Miss Dodge:

Colonel Philip Eubank
Secretary to the President
The White House
Washington, D.C. 20500
Dear Colonel Eubank:

Mr. Randolph Fuller
Press Secretary to the President
The White House
Washington, D.C. 20500

Dear Mr. Fuller:

### 1. Cabinet Officers

The Attorney General receives the salutation of the office.

Attorney General Thomas Cartwright
Department of Justice
Constitution Avenue and 10 Street N.W.
Washington, D.C. 20530

Dear Mr. Attorney General:

Whether other cabinet officers are addressed as **Honorable** is optional. Their salutation is **Dear Mr.** or **Dear Madam Secretary**.

Mr. John Asbury
Secretary of the Treasury
Treasury Department
15 Street and Pennsylvania Avenue N.W.
Washington, D.C. 20220

Dear Mr. Secretary:

Honorable Jane Breckenridge
Secretary of State
Department of State
2201 C Street, N.W.
Washington, D.C. 20520

Dear Madam Secretary:

An under secretary may be addressed as **Honorable**, but the salutation includes no title.

Honorable Vernon Devonshire
Under Secretary of Agriculture
Department of Agriculture
14 Street and Independence Avenue S.W.
Washington, D.C. 20250

Dear Mr. Devonshire:

## 2. Members of Congress

Members and former members of the House of Representatives are addressed as **Honorable** or not, as you prefer. The salutation for present members is **Congressman** or **Congresswoman**, and former members are addressed as **Mr., Mrs.,** or **Miss**.

Honorable W.W. Endicott
House of Representatives
Washington, D.C. 20515

Dear Congressman Endicott:

Representative Alice R. Farrell
House of Representatives
Washington, D.C. 20515

Dear Congresswoman Farrell:

A resident commissioner or delegate is addressed by title and is saluted as **Mr., Mrs.,** or **Miss**.

Honorable Carla C. Jorges
Resident Commissioner of Puerto Rico
(or Delegate of Puerto Rico)
House of Representatives
Washington, D.C. 20515

Dear Mrs. Jorges:

The Speaker of the House of Representatives is addressed as **Mr. Speaker**, but does not retain the title after retiring.

Honorable Edward Hillyer
Speaker of the House of Representatives
Washington, D.C. 20515

Dear Mr. Speaker (or Dear Mr. Hillyer):

Senators, senators-elect, and former senators are addressed as **Honorable** or not, as you prefer. The title **Senator**, however, belongs only to one who is presently serving in the Senate.

Honorable D.D. Jellicoe
United States Senate
Washington, D.C. 20515

Dear Senator Jellicoe:

Senator E. R. Kelland
United States Senate
Washington, D.C. 20515
Dear Senator Kelland:

Honorable Frances Lewis
Senator-elect
United States Senate
Washington, D.C. 20515
Dear Mrs. Lewis:

Honorable Giles Monterey
(local address)
Dear Mr. Monterey:

A Committee chairman is addressed and saluted by the title
of **Chairman**.

Honorable Henry Noble, Chairman
Ways and Means Committee
United States Senate
Washington, D.C. 20515
Dear Mr. Chairman:

Senator Henry Noble, Chairman
Ways and Means Committee
United States Senate
Washington, D.C. 20515
Dear Mr. Chairman:

### 3. Other Federal Officials

The Comptroller General is so addressed.

Honorable Sidney Nichols
Comptroller General of the United States
Washington, D.C. 20548
Dear Mr. Nichols:

The Postmaster General is addressed and saluted by his title.

Honorable Thomas Cartwright
The Postmaster General
U.S. Postal Service
1200 Pennsylvania Avenue N.W.
Washington, D.C. 20260

Dear Mr. Postmaster General:

The Librarian of Congress is addressed just that way.

Honorable Martha Oppenheim
Librarian of Congress
Washington, D.C. 20540

Dear Miss Oppenheim:

Heads or directors of independent agencies are addressed as **Honorable** or **Mr.**, **Mrs.**, and **Miss**, and can be saluted with or without their titles.

Honorable Kurt Pelham, Director
United States Information Agency
1750 Pennsylvania Avenue N.W.
Washington, D.C. 20547

Dear Mr. Director:

Mr. Joseph C. Rogers, Chairman
Indian Claims Commission
1730 E. Street N.W.
Washington, D.C. 20006

Dear Chairman Rogers:

Honorable Jane Sutter, Chairman
Civil Service Commission
1900 E. Street N.W.
Washington, D.C. 20415

Dear Mrs. Sutter:

The Government Printing Office produces many interesting booklets on a wide range of subjects. The head of the office is called the Public Printer, and he may be addressed as **Honorable**.

Honorable Terence Taylor
Public Printer
Government Printing Office
North Capitol and H Streets N.W.
Washington, D.C. 20401

Dear Mr. Taylor:

### 4. Ambassadors, Ministers, and Consuls

An ambassador is addressed either at his embassy in a foreign country or at the State Department in Washington. An ambassador is designated as **Honorable** and is saluted as **Ambassador**.

Honorable Albert Zorach
Ambassador of the United States of America
American Embassy
Moscow, USSR

Dear Mr. Ambassador:

Honorable Shirley Vanderbilt
Ambassador of the United States of America
Department of State
Washington, D.C. 20520

Dear Madam Ambassador (or Dear Mrs. Vanderbilt):

Honorable Thomas Wyeth
Ambassador of the United States of America
American Embassy
London, England

Dear Ambassador Wyeth:

Ministers are addressed in care of the U.S. Legations where they are stationed, and they care called **Honorable** or **Excellency**.

Honorable Martin Allen
Legation of the United States of America
Berlin, West Germany

Dear Mr. Minister:

His Excellency, The American Minister
American Legation
Paris, France

Your Excellency:

A male American consul is given the title of **Esquire**. **Mr.** is never used in conjunction with **Esquire**.

Irving Bliss, Esquire
American Consulate
Bucharest, Rumania

Dear Mr. Bliss:

A female American consul has no title and she is addressed as **Mrs.** or **Miss**.

Miss Isabel Bliss
American Consulate
Bucharest, Rumania

Dear Miss Bliss:

**9:2c** Judicial

The Chief Justice of the U.S. Supreme Court is addressed in either of the following ways:

The Chief Justice
The Supreme Court
Washington, D.C. 20013

Dear Sir:

Honorable James Stanley
Chief Justice of the United States
Washington, D.C. 20013

Dear Mr. Chief Justice:

An associate justice of the U.S. Supreme Court is addressed as follows:

Mr. Justice Edwards
The Supreme Court
Washington, D.C. 20013

Dear Sir:

When a woman becomes a Supreme Court justice, it is planned to drop the **Mr.** in the title and address both sexes simply as **Justice**.

Honorable Albert Edwards
Associate Justice of the Supreme Court of the U.S.
Washington, D.C. 20013

Dear Justice Edwards:

Honorable Alice Edwards
Associate Justice of the Supreme Court of the U.S.
Washington, D.C. 20013

Dear Justice Edwards:

A chief justice of a state supreme court is addressed in either of two ways.

Honorable Barbara Fenway
Chief Justice of the Supreme Court of New York
Albany, New York 12207

Dear Madam Chief Justice (or Dear Judge Fenway):

Honorable Basil Fenway
Chief Justice of the Supreme Court of New York
Albany, New York 12207

Dear Mr. Chief Justice (or Dear Judge Fenway):

A retired justice of the U.S. Supreme Court retains an honorary title.

Honorable Christopher Graham
(local address)

Dear Mr. Justice (or Dear Justice Graham):

All other justices and judges are also addressed as **Honorable**.

Honorable Elbert Jenkins
Judge of the United States District Court for the
Southern District of New Jersey
Princeton, New Jersey 08540

Dear Judge Jenkins:

**9:3** EDUCATIONAL OFFICIALS

Whether a full professor is addressed as **Professor** or **Dr.** depends on the possession of the necessary degree and the professor's personal preference.

Professor Frank Oldenberg
(local address)

Dear Professor Oldenberg:

Grace C. Perkins, Ph.D.
(local address)

Dear Dr. Perkins:

Associate or assistant professors are given the same title in the salutation as full professors.

Mrs. Diana Martin
Associate (Assistant) Professor
Department of Humanities
(local address)

Dear Professor Martin:

Edward Norris, Ph.D.
Associate (Assistant) Professor
Social Studies Department
(local address)

Dear Dr. Norris:

An instructor is not given a title unless he or she possesses a doctorate.

Mr. Henry Rosen
(local address)

Dear Mr. Rosen:

Isaac Shestov, Ph.D.
(local address)

Dear Dr. Shestov:

Deans and assistant deans all get the same salutation, although they may be called **Dr.** in the address.

Dean John C. Thomas
(local address)

Dear Dean Thomas:

Dr. Michael Unger, Dean (Assistant Dean)
(local address)

Dear Dean Unger:

Dean Norma Vanderlyn
(local address)

Dear Dean Vanderlyn:

The president of a college or university receives the salutation of either **Dr.** or **President**.

Osgood Wyman, L.L.D., Ph.D. (or Dr. Osgood Wyman)
President, Pace College
(local address)

Dear Dr. Wyman (or Dear President Wyman):

A college president who is a Catholic priest is addressed as **The Very Reverend** and is saluted as **Father**.

The Very Reverend Paul Yaeger, President
Duquesne University
Pittsburgh, Pennsylvania 15219

Dear Father Yaeger:

A university chancellor is usually a **Dr.** and is addressed by that title.

Dr. Brandon Atwood, Chancellor
University of Hartford
West Hartford, Connecticut 06107

Dear Dr. Atwood:

High school principals are addressed as **Dr.** if they possess a doctor's degree and indicate it in their correspondence. Otherwise, they are **Mr.**, **Mrs.**, or **Miss**.

Dr. George Caldwell, Principal
Mamaroneck High School
Mamaroneck, New York 10543

Dear Dr. Caldwell:

George Caldwell, Ph.D.
Principal, Mamaroneck High School
Mamaroneck, New York 10543

Dear Dr. Caldwell:

Miss Harriet Dyer, Principal
Montclair High School
Montclair, New Jersey 07042

Dear Miss Dyer:

## 9:4 MILITARY PERSONNEL

A general's precise rank is designated in the address. In the salutation, all generals of whatever rank are **Dear General** or **Dear Sir**.

General of the Army, Donald D. Eisler, U.S.A.
(local address)

Dear General Eisler:

General Edgar Fullbright, U.S.A. (or, Brigadier General, Lieutenant General, Major General)
(local address)

Dear General Fullbright:

A colonel or lieutenant colonel receives the salutation of **Colonel**. His rank is indicated in the address.

Colonel (Lieutenant Colonel) Frank Gideon, U.S.A.
(local address)

Dear Colonel Gideon:

An army lieutenant is addressed and saluted in the same way, whether he is a first or second lieutenant.

Lieutenant George G. Hollister, U.S.A.
(local address)

Dear Lieutenant Hollister:

Army majors and captains are addressed and saluted by their titles.

Major Henry Inness, U.S.A.
(local address)

Dear Major Inness:

Captain Isabel Jacobs
(local address)

Dear Captain Jacobs:

An army chaplain is addressed and saluted as **Chaplain**, with his rank of captain following his name in the address. A Catholic chaplain may be saluted as **Father**.

Chaplain James E. Keller, Captain U.S.A.
(local address)

Dear Chaplain Keller:

Chaplain Joseph J. Lowe, Captain U.S.A.
(local address)

Dear Father Lowe:

Army or navy warrant officers or flight officers are addressed as **Mr.**, with the initials after their names indicating the branch of the service.

Marine Corps titles are the same as those in the army except that the top rank is **Commandant of the Marine Corps** and the initials **U.S.M.C.** follow the name.

Air Force address is the same as the army, except that the names are followed by the initials **U.S.A.F.**

Noncommissioned officers in any branch of the service are addressed by their titles, which are also used in the salutation.

Sergeant Joseph Williams, U.S.A.
(local address)

Dear Sergeant Williams:

**9:4a** Naval Personnel

Admirals of the navy must be addressed precisely by their full titles, although all are saluted as **Admiral** or **Dear Sir**.

Fleet Admiral Manuel N. Norton, U.S.N.
Chief of Naval Operations
Department of the Navy
Washington, D.C. 20350

Dear Admiral Norton:

Admiral Herbert H. Oppenheim, U.S.N. (or Vice Admiral, Rear Admiral)
(local address)

Dear Admiral Oppenheim:

Commodores are addressed and saluted by their titles.

Commodore Peter J. Quezon, U.S.N.
(local address)

Dear Commodore Quezon:

Commanders are addressed as **Commander** and saluted as **Commander** or **Dear Sir**.

Commander Oliver S. Patton, U.S.N.
(local address)

Dear Commander Patton:

All naval personnel from **Lieutenant Commander** on down are addressed and saluted by their titles, although junior officers may be saluted as **Mr.**

Lieutenant Commander James J. Revlon, U.S.N.
(local address)

Dear Commander Revlon:

Captain Kenneth Southwick, U.S.N.
(local address)

Dear Captain Southwick

Lieutenant (Lieutenant Junior Grade) Craig L. Trumbull, U.S.N.
(local address)

Dear Mr. Trumbull:

The naval chaplain is addressed as **Chaplain**, with his rank following his name.

Chaplain Thomas J. Villard, Captain U.S.N.
(local address)

Dear Chaplain Villard:

Coast Guard titles are the same as those in the navy, except that the top rank is **Admiral** and the initials **U.S.C.G.** are used instead of **U.S.N.**

## 9:5 RELIGIOUS DIGNITARIES

The pope is addressed as **His Holiness**.

His Holiness Pope John Paul II
Vatican City
State of Italy

Your Holiness (or Most Holy Father):

Other religious dignitaries of the Catholic, Protestant, and Jewish faiths, are addressed as follows:

### 1. Catholic

An apostolic delegate is addressed as **His Excellency**.

His Excellency, The Most Reverend Michael Gilroy
Archbishop of Dublin
The Apostolic Delegate
Washington, D.C. 20013

Your Excellency (or My dear Archbishop):

A United States cardinal is addressed as **His Eminence**. His first name is mentioned before the title **Cardinal**.

His Eminence, George Cardinal Hayes
Archbishop of Chicago
(local address)

Your Eminence:

A Catholic archbishop is addressed as **The Most Reverend** and is saluted as **Your Excellency**.

The Most Reverend Carl C. Jaeger
Archbishop of Detroit
(local address)

Your Excellency:

A Catholic bishop is addressed as **The Most Reverend** and is saluted as **Bishop**.

The Most Reverend Daniel D. Kroll, D.D.
Bishop of Boston
(local address)

Dear Bishop Kroll:

The superior of a community of monks is called an **abbot** and is saluted as **Father**.

The Right Reverend Adam A. Nelligan
Abbot of Prinknash Abbey
Gloucester, England

Dear Father Abbot (or Dear Father Nelligan):

A clergyman belonging to the staff of a cathedral is called a **canon** and is saluted by that title.

The Reverend Francis F. O'Boyle
Canon of Washington Cathedral
(local address)

Dear Canon O'Boyle:

A monsignor is addressed as **The Right Reverend** if he is a local prelate, and **The Very Reverend** if he is a papal chamberlain.

The Right Reverend Monsignor John J. Phillips
(local address)

Right Reverend Monsignor Phillips:

A monk is addressed as **Brother**; a nun is addressed as **Sister**.

Brother Elias E. Rodgers
(local address)

Dear Brother Rodgers:

Sister Maria Theresa
(local address)

Dear Sister Maria Theresa:

A mother superior is addressed as **The Reverend Mother**, followed by the initials of her order.

The Reverend Mother Superior, O.C.A.
(local address)

Dear Reverend Mother (or Dear Mother Superior):

A sister superior is addressed as **The Reverend Sister** and is saluted as **Sister Superior**.

The Reverend Sister Superior
(local address)

Dear Sister Superior:

A superior of a brotherhood is addressed as **The Very Reverend**, followed by the initials of his order. He is saluted as **Father Superior**.

The Very Reverend Joseph Todd, S.F., Director
Monastery of the Franciscan Friars
(local address)

Dear Father Superior:

A Catholic priest with a doctorate is saluted as **Dr.** Otherwise, he is **Father.**

The Reverend Kenneth Venable, Ph.D.
(local address)

Dear Dr. Venable:

The Reverend Lawrence Wylie
(local address)

Dear Father Wylie:

### 2. Protestant

A Protestant archbishop is addressed as **His Grace.**

His Grace
The Lord Archbishop of Canterbury
Canterbury, England

Your Grace (or My Lord Archbishop):

Most other Protestant bishops are addressed as **Bishop** or **The Reverend.**

Bishop Bruce B. Lee, D.D.
(local address)

Dear Bishop Lee:

The Reverend Bruce B. Lee, D.D.
(local address)

Dear Dr. Lee:

A Protestant Episcopal bishop is addressed as **The Right Reverend.**

The Right Reverend John Gifford, D.D.
Bishop of Phoenix
(local address)

Right Reverend Sir (or Dear Bishop Gifford):

An Episcopal priest with a doctor's degree is addressed as **Dr.** Otherwise, he is either **Mr.** or **Father**, and a woman is either **Mrs.** or **Miss.**

The Reverend Saul Ackerman, D.D., Litt.D.
(local address)

Dear Dr. Ackerman (or Dear Father Ackerman):

The Reverend Saul Ackerman
(local address)

Dear Mr. Ackerman (or Dear Father Ackerman):

The Reverend Victoria Benson, D.D.
(local address)

Dear Dr. Benson:

The Reverend Victoria Benson
(local address)

Dear Mrs. Benson:

A Protestant minister with a doctor's degree is saluted as **Dr.** Otherwise, he is called **Mr.** or **Pastor**, and a woman is called **Mrs.** or **Miss**.

The Reverend David Chase, D.D.
(local address)

Dear Dr. Chase:

The Reverend David Chase
(local address)

Dear Mr. Chase (or Dear Pastor Chase):

The Reverend Dorothy Chisholm
(local address)

Dear Miss Chisholm:

### 3. Jewish

A rabbi is addressed as **Dr.** or **Rabbi** when he possesses a doctor's degree. Otherwise, he is **Rabbi**.

Rabbi Isaac Dietrich, Litt.D.
(local address)

Dear Dr. Dietrich:

Rabbi Morris Loeb
(local address)

Dear Rabbi Loeb:

**9:6** FOREIGN AND U.N. ADDRESS

A foreign ambassador in the United States is addressed as **His Excellency** and is saluted as **Excellency** or **Mr. Ambassador.**

His Excellency, Arthur A. Karlson
Ambassador of Sweden
Washington, D.C. 20027
Dear Mr. Ambassador:

A foreign chargé d'affaires in the United States is addressed as **Mr.**

Mr. José J. Rodriguez
Chargé d'Affaires of Chile
Washington, D.C. 20027
Dear Mr. Rodriguez:

A foreign minister in the United States is addressed as **The Honorable** and is saluted as **Mr. Minister.**

The Honorable Lance duLac
Minister of France
Washington, D.C. 20027
Dear Mr. Minister:

A foreign ambassador to the United Nations is addressed as **His Excellency** and is saluted as **Excellency** or **Mr. Ambassador.**

His Excellency, Curtis C. Cabot
Representative of Canada
to the United Nations
New York, New York 10017
Dear Mr. Ambassador:

A United States ambassador to the United Nations is addressed as **The Honorable** and is saluted as **Mr.** or **Madam Ambassador.**

The Honorable Shirley Black
United States Representative to the United Nations
New York, New York 10017
Dear Madam Ambassador:

A United States representative to the United Nations is addressed as **The Honorable** and is saluted as **Mr.**, **Mrs.**, or **Miss**.

The Honorable Gerald G. Gould
Senior Representative of the United States
to the General Assembly of the United Nations
New York, New York 10017

Dear Mr. Gould:

The Secretary General of the United Nations is addressed as **His Excellency** and is saluted as **Excellency** or **Mr. Secretary General**.

His Excellency, Arthur A. Andrews
Secretary General of the United Nations
New York, New York 10017

Dear Mr. Secretary General:

CONCLUSION

In a salutation, it is always wise to include a person's official title, such as **Dear Governor** Jones or **Dear Judge** Smith, as people take pride in the positions they hold.

# 10. WORD DIVISION

Word division should be avoided whenever possible, unless it makes the right-hand margin of the letter too irregular. When you must divide, there are ten simple rules to follow which will make the divided words easier to read.

## 10:1 TEN CONCISE RULES

1. Words of more than two syllables are divided on a vowel, unless such division interferes with correct pronunciation.

abdi-cate       centi-grade
geno-cide       para-noid

But **not**: gala-xy or homo-genize

2. Separate double consonants, unless it means breaking up a root word.

ban-ning        dun-ning
reces-sion      win-ner

But **not**: fil-ling or instal-ling

3. Separate two consonants preceded and followed by vowels.

domes-tic
mis-sile
ren-dered

4. To avoid confusion, hyphenated compounds should be divided at the hyphen and solid compounds should be divided between the two basic words.

| Hyphenated | Solid |
|---|---|
| Latin-American | back-ground |
| self-addressed | age-less |
| above-mentioned | air-wave |

5. Do not divide contractions.

hasn't
wouldn't

6. Never separate the first letter of a word from the rest.

adept
eclipse
icicle
opaque

7. Never divide a four-letter word, and only rarely should you divide a five-letter word.

decoy
defy
lucky
many
pity
idle

8. Do not divide words that are pronounced as one syllable, no matter how many letters are involved.

drought
friend
wrought
schism

9. Avoid the separation of two-letter syllables at the beginnings of words with three or more syllables.

| aspi-rin | **not** | as-pirin |
|---|---|---|
| inten-tion | **not** | in-tention |
| unfor-tunate | **not** | un-fortunate |

10. Do not divide words at the ends of two successive lines, and never divide the last word in a paragraph.

## 10:2 PROPER NAMES

Do not divide proper nouns if it can be avoided, especially the names of persons, and never separate the initials from the rest of the name.

When division of proper names cannot be avoided, follow the general rules.

| | |
|---|---|
| Abra-ham | Cleo-patra |
| Man-hattan | Lon-don |
| B. Alt-man | Rome |
| Adolph | Leo-pold |

## 10:3 PREFIXES

A prefix is a syllable that is put before a word and changes its meaning. Such a word is usually divided on the prefix, although it is preferable not to separate a two-letter prefix.

### 10:3a Three-Letter Prefix

Words with three-letter prefixes can usually be divided conveniently on the prefix.

dis-color
pre-dominant
pro-cession

### 10:3b Two-Syllable Prefix

Prefixes of more than one syllable are usually preserved intact, to make the meaning clear.

| | |
|---|---|
| ante | multi |
| anti | over |
| hyper | poly |
| inter | retro |
| macro | semi |
| micro | ultra |

### 10:3c Two-Letter Prefix

Although it should be avoided whenever possible, words with two-letter prefixes can be divided on the prefix when absolutely necessary.

| | |
|---|---|
| ab-sent | in-duce |
| ad-verb | ob-ject |
| de-cline | re-store |
| de-scribe | un-happy |

## 10:4 SUFFIXES

Suffixes are added to the ends of base words to modify the meaning or change the usage.

### 10:4a Avoiding Two-Letter Carryovers

The carrying over of two-letter endings should be avoided, especially in words of more than three syllables.

| | | |
|---|---|---|
| instabil-ity | **not** | instabili-ty |
| adver-tiser | **not** | advertis-er |
| vegetar-ian | **not** | vegetari-an |

**Exception**: A sounded **ed** ending can be carried over.

| | | |
|---|---|---|
| inflat-ed | but **never** | propos-ed |

### 10:4b Division of Two-Letter Carryovers

There are instances when two-letter carryovers cannot be avoided, because the root word would be improperly broken up.

| | | |
|---|---|---|
| announc-er | **not** | announ-cer |
| examin-er | **not** | exami-ner |
| observ-er | **not** | obser-ver |

**Exception:** Words ending in **or**, with a preceding consonant, are usually divided before the consonant.

administra-tor
counse-lor
supervi-sor

## 10:4c  IBLE and ABLE

The suffixes **able** and **ible** are usually carried over complete in themselves.

compat-ible     collaps-ible
predict-able     fashion-able

**Exceptions:**

inflam-mable
memo-rable
irrespon-sible

## 10:4d  Positively Indivisible Suffixes

Some suffixes cannot be broken up under any circumstances.

commer-cial     ini-tial     controver-sial
suspi-cion     ten-sion     igni-tion
gra-cious     preten-tious     herba-ceous
gor-geous     reli-gious     re-gion

## 10:4e  The ING Suffix

Words ending in **ing** are divided on the base word, unless the final consonant is doubled.

enlist-ing     report-ing     review-ing
omit-ting     infer-ring     get-ting

**Exception:** When the word ends in a silent vowel preceded by two consonants, the final consonant or consonants become part of the suffix.

trou-bling
bun-dling
med-dling
trick-ling

### 10:4f The METER Suffix

When **meter** is pronounced with a long **e** as in **kilometer**, the suffix **meter** is not divided.

kilo-meter
centi-meter
milli-meter

**Exception:** When it is pronounced with a short **e**, as in **speed-ometer**, the division comes after the **m**.

speedom-eter
barom-eter
thermom-eter

### 10:4g Plural Endings

Plural endings of **es** should not be carried over alone, unless it would break up a word awkwardly.

|       | hor-ses  | ten-ses |
|-------|----------|---------|
| **but** | gross-es | rich-es |

### 10:5 WORD DIVISION TEST

1. Which of the following divisions of the word **duplicate** is correct?

   a. du-plicate
   b. duplic-ate
   c. dupli-cate

2. How would you divide **centered**?

3. Where would you separate **centerpiece**?

4. Which of the following are correct?

   a. ham-mer
   b. progress-ive
   c. install-ing
   d. proces-sing

5. How would you divide the following?
   a. doesn't
   b. haven't
   c. thought
   d. frowned
   e. only

6. What is the correct division of these words?
   a. antidote
   b. discussion
   c. overcome
   d. debated

7. Where would you divide these suffixes?
   a. disciplinarian
   b. adviser
   c. guarantor

8. Which of the following is incorrectly divided?
   a. comfort-able
   b. formid-able
   c. dura-ble
   d. manage-able

9. Pick out the wrong division among the following:
   a. expan-sion
   b. recogni-tion
   c. essen-tial
   d. provinc-ial
   e. deli-cious

10. What is wrong with the word divisions in this paragraph?

   Although we cannot extend credit privileges
at the present time, we would be happy to ship merchandise to you on C.O.D. terms. Perhaps in the future, if you try us again, we may be able to recon-
sider.

(The answers to this test are at the end of the chapter.)

## 10:6 TWO-SYLLABLE WORD DIVISION LIST

Words of two syllables are split at the end of the first syllable, as indicated in this typical list.

**A**

ab·duct
ab·rupt
ab·sent
ac·cent
ac·tor
ad·age
ad·mire
af·firm
af·ter
ag·ile
al·bum
al·ter
am·bush
an·chor
an·ger
an·nul
ap·peal
ar·rest
ar·rive
ar·row
art·ist
as·pect
as·tute
at·las
at·tain

**B**

bab·ble
bag·gy
bal·ance
ban·ish
bank·er
bap·tise
bar·ber
ba·sis

beau·ty
be·gin
be·nign
be·quest
bill·board
blan·ket
bla·tant
blink·er
block·ade
bod·ice
bond·age
bo·nus
bor·der
bro·ken
bur·den
bu·reau
bur·glar

**C**

ca·ble
caf·feine
cal·lous
cam·pus
can·cel
can·did
can·dor
can·not
can·vass
ca·reer
cash·ier
ca·ter
cen·sor
cen·sus
cer·tain
chal·lenge
chap·ter

cher·ish
cho·rus
Christ·mas
cir·cuit
clas·sic
cleav·age
cli·max
col·late

**D**

dai·ly
dam·age
Dan·ish
dar·ing
de·bate
debt·or
dec·ade
de·fer
de·gree
del·uge
den·tal
de·rive
des·pot
de·tain
de·tect
dic·tate
dif·fer
di·rect
dis·bar
dis·burse
dis·cuss
di·vide
dol·lar
doz·en
driv·en

**E**

ear·nest
ea·sel
ef·fect
ef·fort
eight·een
ei·ther
el·bow
em·bark
em·blem
em·pire
em·ploy
en·chant
en·close
en·dorse
en·roll
ep·och
er·mine
er·rand
er·ror
es·cape
es·say
es·trange
eth·ics
eth·nic
ex·act

**F**

fab·ric
fac·et
fac·tion
fac·tor
fail·ure
far·ther
fash·ion
fa·tigue

fa-vor
fea-ture
feed-back
fel-low
fe-male
fer-tile
fes-tive
fi-ber
fic-tion
fig-ure
fil-ter
fix-ture
fla-grant
flip-pant
flour-ish
flu-ent
frac-tion

**G**

gal-ley
gal-lon
ga-lore
gam-ble
gar-nish
gas-tric
gen-der
ge-nial
ge-nius
gent-ly
ges-ture
gi-ant
glar-ing
glob-al
glos-sy
gold-en
gor-geous
gos-pel
gos-sip
gour-met
grate-ful
gri-mace
gro-tesque

grue-some
gus-to

**H**

hab-it
hal-ter
ham-per
hand-some
har-ass
har-ness
haz-ard
health-ful
heav-en
hel-met
hence-forth
her-mit
her-self
hey-day
hid-den
hin-drance
hob-by
hock-ey
hold-er
hol-low
hon-or
hook-up
hos-tage
hu-man
hus-band


**I**

ig-nite
ig-nore
im-age
im-bibe
im-mense
im-pede
im-ply
in-ane
in-born
in-cline

in-dex
in-fringe
in-vite
irk-some
is-land
is-sue
it-self

**J**

jack-et
jar-gon
jew-el
jock-ey
jos-tle
jour-ney
joy-ful
jum-bo
jus-tice

**K**

ka-pok
ken-nel
ker-nel
kid-nap
kind-ly
knowl-edge
knuck-le
ku-dos

**L**

la-bor
lac-quer
la-ment
lam-poon
lan-guage
lan-tern
large-ly
lar-ynx
la-tent
laun-der
lav-ish
leak-age

leath-er
lec-ture
ledg-er
le-gal
leg-end
lei-sure
le-thal
li-cense
lim-it
lin-guist
liq-uid
lis-ten
lo-cal
log-ic
look-out
lum-ber
lunch-eon
lus-cious
lyr-ic


**M**

ma-chine
mag-ic
mag-net
main-tain
ma-jor
mal-ice
ma-lign
mam-moth
man-age
man-ner
mar-gin
mar-ket
mar-riage
mas-cot
mas-sage
match-less
ma-tron
mat-ter
ma-ture
meas-ure

med-al
mem-oir
men-tion
mer-cy
mes-sage
mi-grate
mil-lion
mi-nor
mo-lest
mon-ey
mor-al
mor-bid
muf-fle

**N**

na-ive
nap-kin
nar-rate
na-tive
na-ture
neck-lace
nee-dle
neg-lect
nei-ther
neph-ew
neu-tral
nick-el
non-sense
nor-mal
note-book
no-tice
no-tion
nour-ish
nov-ice
nui-sance
num-ber
nup-tial
nur-ture
nut-shell
ny-lon

**O**

oat-meal
ob-ject
ob-long
ob-scene
ob-scure
oc-cult
oc-cur
oc-tave
of-fend
of-fer
of-fice
of-ten
on-set
op-pose
op-press
op-tion
or-ange
or-bit
or-der
or-nate
or-phan
os-trich
oth-er
own-er

**P**

pack-age
pad-lock
pag-eant
pal-ace
pal-ate
pal-lid
pam-per
pam-phlet
pan-der
pan-el
pan-ic
pa-per
pa-rade

par-cel
par-don
par-ent
par-lor
part-ner
pas-sage
pat-ent
pa-tron
pe-nal
pen-ance
pen-sion
peo-ple
per-ceive
per-form
per-son
pho-to
pick-et
pic-nic
pic-ture
pin-point
pi-rate
pit-fall
pla-cate
plain-tiff
plas-tic
pleas-ant
plu-ral
po-lite
pol-lute
por-trait
pos-sess
pos-ture
pre-cede
pri-vate
pro-claim
pur-pose

**Q**

quag-mire
Quak-er

quar-rel
quar-ter
que-ry
quib-ble
qui-et
quin-tet
quo-rum

**R**

rab-bit
ra-cial
ra-cism
ra-dar
ran-cor
rau-cous
re-act
rea-son
re-bate
re-cap
re-ceipt
re-cent
re-cord (v.)
rec-ord (n.)
re-deem
ref-uge
re-gret
re-ject
ren-der
re-new
rent-al
re-pair
re-place
re-ply
re-port
rep-tile
re-quest
re-serve
res-pite
re-sponse
re-tail

| | | | |
|---|---|---|---|
| re-vise | sor-ry | through-out | vir-tue |
| rig-id | spe-cial | ti-rade | vi-sion |
| ros-trum | squan-der | ti-tle | |
| ro-tate | squeam-ish | top-ic | **W** |
| ruf-fle | stand-ard | to-tal | wa-ger |
| rup-ture | stat-ute | trac-tion | wait-ress |
| ruth-less | sten-cil | tran-scend | wak-en |
| | strin-gent | tran-scribe | warn-ing |
| **S** | struc-ture | trans-fer | waste-ful |
| sa-cred | sub-ject | trans-pose | wel-come |
| safe-ty | sub-mit | trau-ma | wheth-er |
| sa-lute | sub-stance | trus-tee | wid-ow |
| sanc-tion | sub-tle | typ-ist | will-ful |
| sat-ire | sum-mon | | wis-dom |
| sav-age | su-preme | **U** | wish-ful |
| scan-dal | symp-tom | ul-cer | wit-ness |
| schol-ar | | un-der | wom-an |
| sci-ence | **T** | un-less | won-der |
| scrip-ture | tab-loid | up-ward | wor-ry |
| sea-son | tac-it | ur-gent | writ-ten |
| se-cret | tac-tics | ut-most | |
| seg-ment | tal-ent | | **Y** |
| se-quel | tam-per | **V** | yearn-ing |
| se-ries | tar-get | va-cant | yon-der |
| shel-ter | tem-per | val-id | youth-ful |
| short-age | ten-ant | van-ish | |
| sig-nal | ten-sion | ven-ture | **Z** |
| sim-ple | tex-ture | ver-bose | zeal-ous |
| slan-der | ther-mal | ver-sus | ze-nith |
| so-ber | the-sis | vi-brate | zip-per |
| som-ber | thou-sand | vic-tim | |

## 10:7 THREE-SYLLABLE WORD DIVISION LIST

Words of three syllables are ordinarily divided on the vowel, but there are many other factors involved. If you stop to pronounce the word, the division will usually be obvious.

**Vowel:** fugi-tive    barri-cade    cere-al
**Other:** aban-don    deben-ture    effec-tive

# A

abdi-cate
abdo-men
abey-ance
abnor-mal
abol-ish
abro-gate
acci-dent
accli-mate
accom-plish
accred-it
accu-rate
accus-tom
acknowl-edge
actu-al
addi-tion
ade-quate
adjec-tive
admis-sion
advan-tage
adver-tise
advo-cate
affec-tion
agen-da
aggra-vate
aggre-gate
alco-hol
alli-ance
alma-nac
alter-nate
ambi-tion
anno-tate
appar-ent
appre-hend
aque-duct
arbi-trate
ascer-tain
atten-tion
audi-ence
aver-age

# B

bache-lor
bank-ruptcy
bear-able
bicy-cle
bind-ery
biweek-ly
blandish-ment
body-guard
book-keeper
broad-cast
broker-age
bulle-tin
busi-ness

# C

Cadil-lac
calcu-late
calen-dar
cam-era
capa-cious
capi-tal
carni-val
casi-no
cata-lyst
celi-bate
cen-tury
cer-tify
chan-cellor
chap-eron
char-acter
charis-ma
chloro-form
chro-mium
circu-lar
circum-stance
clas-sify
cogni-zant
colos-sal
commer-cial
compan-ion

com-pensate
compe-tence
compli-cate
compro-mise
concen-trate
conde-scend
condi-tion
conse-quence
con-sider
consum-mate
contem-plate
contra-dict
conver-sion
corpo-rate
coura-geous
cred-ible
cubi-cle
cur-sory
cus-tomer
cylin-der

# D

deben-ture
decep-tion
deci-sive
deco-rum
dedi-cate
defi-cit
dehy-drate
delin-quent
demar-cate
depos-it
depre-cate
depres-sion
desig-nate
deter-gent
devi-ate
diag-nose
dia-gram
differ-ence
diffi-cult

disci-pline
dispos-sess
diver-sion
docu-ment
dupli-cate

# E

eccen-tric
edu-cate
effi-cient
elec-tric
elo-quence
embez-zle
emi-nence
empha-sis
encom-pass
engen-der
enor-mous
epi-gram
eru-dite
estab-lish
eti-quette
euphe-mism
evi-dence
exam-ine
excur-sion
exe-cute
exer-cise
ex-hibit
expe-dite
explo-sion
extra-dite

# F

fabri-cate
face-tious
feasi-ble
femi-nine
fero-cious
ficti-tious
flabber-gast

flex·ible
fluctu·ate
for·ever
formal·ize
formu·late
forti·tude
frater·nal
frivo·lous
furstra·tion
furni·ture
fuse·lage

## G

gal·axy
galva·nize
garru·lous
gen·eral
genu·ine
gigan·tic
glos·sary
govern·ment
gradu·ate
grati·tude
guaran·tee
gyro·scope

## H

handi·cap
haphaz·ard
hemi·sphere
hesi·tate
holi·ness
homi·cide
hori·zon
hospi·tal
how·ever
hurri·cane
hydrau·lic
hydro·gen
hypno·sis

## I

idi·om
ille·gal
illu·sive
imag·ine
imma·ture
immi·grate
impair·ment
impar·tial
impend·ing
impe·tus
imple·ment
impos·tor
impro·vise
incen·tive
inci·dent
incom·plete
incor·rect
incum·bent
indi·cate
indus·try
iner·tia
infil·trate
influ·ence
ingen·ious
inhu·man
injus·tice
inno·vate
insin·cere
insti·tute
insu·late
irri·tate
iso·late

## J

jani·tor
jeop·ardy
judi·cial
juve·nile

## K

kine·scope
know·ingly

## L

laby·rinth
lami·nate
lassi·tude
lati·tude
legi·ble
legis·late
lever·age
licen·tious
limit·less
liqui·date
liter·ate
litho·graph
longi·tude
loqua·cious
lubri·cate
lucra·tive

## M

macro·cosm
maga·zine
malcon·tent
mali·cious
maneu·ver
mani·fest
mara·thon
mascu·line
matri·arch
maxi·mum
medi·ate
mesmer·ize
meta·phor
micro·phone
mini·mum
miscon·strue
moder·ate
modi·cum

modu·late
momen·tous
mono·logue
moti·vate
multi·ply
muti·late

## N

natu·ral
navi·gate
nebu·lous
negli·gent
neuro·sis
nico·tine
nitro·gen
noctur·nal
nomi·nal
noncha·lant
nota·tion
Novem·ber
numer·ous
nutri·ent

## O

obli·gate
obnox·ious
obso·lete
occa·sion
occu·pant
odi·ous
offi·cial
oper·ate
opin·ion
oppor·tune
opti·mum
ordi·nance
orna·ment
ostra·cize
ova·tion
over·draft
owner·ship

**P**

pala·tial
pali·sade
palpi·tate
panto·mime
para·digm
paral·lel
para·phrase
parti·san
pater·nal
patri·cian
pecul·iar
pedes·tal
pene·trate
percep·tive
perfo·rate
perma·nent
permis·sion
perpe·trate
pessi·mist
photo·graph
physi·cal
pictur·esque
pinna·cle
piti·less
plati·tude
plausi·ble
plebe·ian
polar·ize
popu·lar
poten·tial
practi·cal
preco·cious
preju·dice
prema·ture
presi·dent
previ·ous
procre·ate
prodi·gious
profes·sion
propi·tious

prose·cute
provi·sion
psycho·sis
publi·cize

**Q**

quadru·ped
quadru·ple
quaran·tine
queru·lous
quintes·sence

**R**

racon·teur
radi·ant
read·able
reaf·firm
real·ize
rebut·tal
recep·tion
recog·nize
recon·cile
redun·dant
refresh·ment
regi·ment
regis·ter
regu·late
rela·tive
reli·ant
remem·ber
reno·vate
reper·toire
repos·sess
repre·sent
repro·duce
requi·site
respon·sive
retro·spect
reve·nue
ridi·cule
rudi·ment

ruin·ous
rumi·nate

**S**

sacra·ment
sacri·fice
sacro·sanct
satel·lite
sati·ate
satu·rate
scholas·tic
scintil·late
seces·sion
secu·lar
seda·tion
segre·gate
seman·tics
sensa·tion
sepa·rate
sever·ance
signa·ture
simi·lar
sine·cure
singu·lar
skele·ton
soli·taire
solu·tion
sopho·more
souve·nir
speci·men
specu·late
statis·tics
stimu·late
strenu·ous
stupen·dous
subcon·scious
subli·mate
submis·sion
subse·quent
substand·ard
subter·fuge

suffi·cient
sum·mary
supe·rior
super·sede
surro·gate
surveil·lance

**T**

tabu·late
tangi·ble
tanta·mount
tedi·ous
tele·cast
tele·type
tena·cious
tenta·tive
termi·nate
thermo·stat
titil·late
toler·ant
topi·cal
tourna·ment
tracta·ble
trans·action
trans·fusion
trans·parent
treas·urer
trium·phant
turbu·lent

**U**

ulti·mate
uncom·mon
under·neath
unfaith·ful
unfas·ten
union·ize
uni·verse
unti·tled
uti·lize

| V | W |
|---|---|
| vaca-tion | who-ever |
| vacil-late | wilder-ness |
| vari-ous | with-drawal |
| vindi-cate | wonder-ful |
| voca-tion | workman-ship |
| vola-tile | |
| volun-teer | |

## Answers to Word Division Test

1. c
2. cen-tered
3. center-piece
4. a and c
5. Do not divide any.
6. anti-dote       over-come
   discus-sion     debat-ed
7. disciplinar-ian, advis-er, guaran-tor
8. b. It should be **formidable** or **formida-ble**
9. d. It should be **provin-cial**
10. Words are divided at the end of two successive lines, followed by the division of the final word of the paragraph. This would look better:

    Athough we cannot extend credit privileges at the present time, we would be happy to ship merchandise to you on C.O.D. terms. Perhaps in the future, if you try us again, we may be able to reconsider.

## CONCLUSION

Keep your margins neat and hyphenate only when you must; the fewer broken words, the better.

# 11. ABBREVIATIONS

In a business letter, it shows poor taste to abbreviate ordinary words like **received**, **department**, or **month**, even though your correspondent will know the meaning of **rec'd, dept.,** and **mo.** There are, however, many words that are abbreviated by custom, like **Mister (Mr.)**, **post meridiem (p.m.)**, and **cash on delivery (c.o.d.)**. In addition, abbreviations like **NATO, OPEC,** and **ICBM** have become part of our current language.

## 11:1 WHERE TO AVOID

1. Never abbreviate the name of a month, even in the heading of a letter.

September 14, 198-
Your letter of January 4

2. Always spell out **Reverend, Honorable, Senator, President,** and **Professor,** as well as military titles.

| | |
|---|---|
| Reverend Cecil Connelly | Honorable David Dickens |
| Senator Elbert Keane | Mr. Edward Evans, President |
| Professor George Eliot | Colonel Frank Field |

**Doctor** may be abbreviated to **Dr.**

Dr. Henry Higgins

3. Do not abbreviate first names of persons unless they do so in their signatures.

Frederick M. Foster **not** Fred M. Foster

4. Avoid colloquial abbreviations like **lab** for **laboratory, info** for **information,** and **steno** for **stenographer** or **stenography.**

5. Abbreviations like **Co.** for **company,** and **No.** for **number,**

are permissible in combination with other terms, but not when used alone.

You have a **number** of models to choose from.
This is our model **No.** 1234.
You are invited to the **company** outing.
We purchased the material from J. Jones & **Co.**

## 11:2 MEASUREMENTS—NEW METRIC AND U.S. STANDARD

Measurements of any kind are not abbreviated in the body of a letter, but in orders or invoices and lists or tables they may be abbreviated to save time and space.

### Metric System

| | | |
|---|---|---|
| LENGTH | myriameter | mym |
| | kilometer | km |
| | hectometer | hm |
| | decameter | dkm |
| | meter | m |
| | decimeter | dm |
| | centimeter | cm |
| | millimeter | mm |
| AREA | square kilometer | $km^2$ |
| | hectare | ha |
| | are | a |
| | centare | ca |
| | square centimeter | $cm^2$ |
| | square meter | $m^2$ |
| MASS | metric ton | MT |
| & | quintal | q |
| WEIGHT | kilogram | kg |
| | hectogram | hg |
| | decagram | dkg |
| | gram | g |
| | decigram | dg |
| | centigram | cg |
| | milligram | mg |
| VOLUME | cubic centimeter | cc **or** $cm^3$ |
| | stere | s |

| CAPACITY | kiloliter | kl |
|---|---|---|
| | hectoliter | hl |
| | decaliter | dkl |
| | liter | l |
| | deciliter | dl |
| | centiliter | cl |
| | milliliter | ml |
| TEMPERATURE | Celsius | C |
| | centigrade | c |

## U.S. Standard

| LENGTH | mile | mi. |
|---|---|---|
| | rod | rd. |
| | yard | yd. |
| | foot | ft. **or** ' |
| | inch | in. **or** " |
| | square mile | sq. mi. **or** mi.$^2$ |
| | acre | a. |
| | square rod | sq. rd. **or** rd.$^2$ |
| | square foot | sq. ft. **or** ft.$^2$ |
| | square inch | sq. in. **or** in.$^2$ |
| VOLUME | cubic yard | cu. yd. **or** yd.$^3$ |
| | cubic foot | cu. ft. **or** ft.$^3$ |
| | cubic inch. | cu. in. **or** in.$^3$ |
| WEIGHT | ton | tn. |
| | hundredweight | cwt. |
| | pound | lb. |
| | ounce | oz. |
| | dram | dr. |
| | grain | gr. |
| CAPACITY | gallon | gal. |
| LIQUID | quart | qt. |
| | pint | pt. |
| | gill | gi. |
| | fluid ounce | fl. oz. |
| | fluid dram | fl. dr. |
| | minim | min. |
| CAPACITY | bushel | bu. |

| | | |
|---|---|---|
| DRY | peck | pk. |
| | quart | qt. |
| | pint | pt. |
| TEMPERATURE | Fahrenheit | F |

## 11:3 LATEST POSTAL ABBREVIATIONS

In the address of a letter, it is preferable to write out such words as **avenue, street, square,** or **place.** The abbreviations **NW, SW, NE,** and **SE** are used to indicate sections of cities, but the words **North, South, East,** and **West** are always spelled out, as well as the words **county, fort, mount, point,** and **port.**

The name of a city, no matter how long, should not be abbreviated except for use on addressing equipment, in which case you can write **Prt Jefferson** or **Pt Chautauqua.** These spellings must follow the regulations of the U.S. Postal Department, as no other special abbreviations are permitted. You cannot write **Va. Beach** if the Post Office abbreviates it as **Virginia Bch.** All such permissible abbreviations may be obtained from the Post Office Department in Washington, D.C.

### 11:3a State Abbreviations

The traditional abbreviations for states, territories, and possessions of the United States are more attractive than the two-letter abbreviations approved by the Post Office, and a full spelling out of a short state name like **Vermont** or **Kansas** looks better than **Vt.** or **Kans.** With today's zip codes, however, you may need the extra space that abbreviations provide.

#### Two-Letter State Abbreviations

| | | | |
|---|---|---|---|
| Alabama | AL | District | |
| Alaska | AK | of Columbia | DC |
| Arizona | AZ | Florida | FL |
| Arkansas | AR | Georgia | GA |
| California | CA | Guam | GU |
| Colorado | CO | Hawaii | HI |
| Connecticut | CT | Idaho | ID |
| Delaware | DE | Illinois | IL |

| Indiana | IN | North Dakota | ND |
| Iowa | IA | Ohio | OH |
| Kansas | KS | Oklahoma | OK |
| Kentucky | KY | Oregon | OR |
| Louisiana | LA | Pennsylvania | PA |
| Maine | ME | Puerto Rico | PR |
| Maryland | MD | Rhode Island | RI |
| Massachusetts | MA | South Carolina | SC |
| Michigan | MI | South Dakota | SD |
| Minnesota | MN | Tennessee | TN |
| Mississippi | MS | Texas | TX |
| Missouri | MO | Utah | UT |
| Montana | MT | Vermont | VT |
| Nebraska | NE | Virginia | VA |
| Nevada | NV | Virgin | |
| New Hampshire | NH | Islands | VI |
| New Jersey | NJ | Washington | WA |
| New Mexico | NM | West Virginia | WV |
| New York | NY | Wisconsin | WI |
| North Carolina | NC | Wyoming | WY |

## Traditional State Abbreviations

| Alabama | Ala. | Indiana | Ind. |
| Alaska | Alaska | Iowa | Iowa |
| Arizona | Ariz. | Kansas | Kans. |
| Arkansas | Ark. | Kentucky | Ky. |
| California | Calif. | Louisiana | La. |
| Canal Zone | C.Z. | Maine | Maine |
| Colorado | Colo. | Maryland | Md. |
| Connecticut | Conn. | Massachusetts | Mass. |
| Delaware | Del. | Michigan | Mich. |
| District of | | Minnesota | Minn. |
| Columbia | D.C. | Mississippi | Miss. |
| Florida | Fla. | Missouri | Mo. |
| Georgia | Ga. | Montana | Mont. |
| Guam | Guam | Nebraska | Nebr. |
| Hawaii | Hawaii | Nevada | Nev. |
| Idaho | Idaho | New Hampshire | N.H. |
| Illinois | Ill. | New Jersey | N.J. |

| | | | |
|---|---|---|---|
| New Mexico | N. Mex. | South Dakota | S.Dak. |
| New York | N.Y. | Tennessee | Tenn. |
| North Carolina | N.C. | Texas | Tex. |
| North Dakota | N. Dak. | Utah | Utah |
| Ohio | Ohio | Vermont | Vt. |
| Oklahoma | Okla. | Virginia | Va. |
| Oregon | Oreg. | Virgin Islands | V.i. |
| Pennsylvania | Pa. | Washington | Wash. |
| Puerto Rico | P.R. | West Virginia | W.Va. |
| Rhode Island | R.I. | Wisconsin | Wis. |
| Samoa | Samoa | Wyoming | Wyo. |
| South Carolina | S.C. | | |

## 11:4 BUSINESS AND TECHNICAL TERMS

Avoid abbreviations whenever possible, but when you must use them, the following are standard:

**A**

| | |
|---|---|
| abridged | abr. |
| account current | A/C |
| account of | a/o |
| accounts payable | A/cs Pay. |
| accounts receivable | A/cs Rec. |
| actual weight | A/W |
| additional premium | A/P |
| ad infinitum | ad inf. |
| ad libitum | ad lib. |
| ad locum | ad loc. |
| administration | admin. |
| administrator | admr. |
| administratrix | admx. |
| ad valorem | ad val., A/V |
| advertisement | advt., ad |
| affidavit | afft. |
| affirmed | aff'd |
| after date | a/d |
| afternoon | p. m. |
| against all risks | a. a. r. |

| | |
|---|---|
| agent, agreement | agt. |
| a good brand | a. g. b. |
| all risks | A/R |
| alternating current | A. C. |
| amended | amd. |
| American terms | A/T |
| American wire gauge | A. W. G. |
| amount | amt. |
| ampere(s) | amp. |
| ampere-hours | a-h |
| amplitude modulation | AM |
| angstrom unit(s) | A |
| anonymous | anon. |
| answer, answered | ans. |
| approved | appd. |
| approximately | approx. |
| arrival notice | a. n. |
| article | art. |
| assessment | assmt. |
| assessment paid | Apd. |
| assignment | assigt. |
| assistant | asst. |
| association | assn., ass'n |
| at (price) | @ |
| Atlantic Standard Time | A. S. T. |
| atomic weight | at. wt. |
| at sight | a. s. |
| attached to other corres. | A. to O. C. |
| attorney | atty. |
| audio frequency | AF |
| authorized version | A. V. |
| average | av. |
| avoirdupois | avdp. |

**B**

| | |
|---|---|
| bail bond | b. b. |
| balance | bal. |
| bale(s) | bl. |
| bank | bk. |
| bank draft | B/D |

| | |
|---|---|
| bank post bill | b. p. b. |
| bankrupt | bkpt. |
| barometer | bar. |
| barrel(s) | bbl. |
| basket(s) | bsk., bkt. |
| before Christ | B. C. |
| before noon | a. m. |
| bibliography | bibliog. |
| bill book | b. b. |
| bill of collection | B/C |
| bill of entry | B/E |
| bill of exchange | B/E |
| bill of health | B/H |
| bill of lading | B/L |
| bill of parcels | B/P |
| bill of sale | B/S |
| bill of sight | B/St. |
| billion electron volts | Bev |
| bills of lading | Bs/L |
| bills payable | B/P |
| bills receivable | B/R |
| biography | biog. |
| biology | biol. |
| Birmingham wire gauge | B. W. G. |
| board feet | Bd. ft. |
| bonded goods | B/G |
| book value | B/v |
| Boulevard | Blvd. |
| box | bx |
| brake horsepower | b. h. p. |
| British thermal unit(s) | b. t. u. |
| brother | Bro. |
| brothers | Bros. |
| brought over | b/o |
| building | bldg. |
| bulletin | bul., bull. |
| business | bus. |
| business manager | Bus. Mgr. |
| buyer's option, back order | b. o. |

# C

| | |
|---|---|
| candlepower | cp |
| capital | cap. |
| capital account | C/A |
| capital letters | caps |
| carat | k. |
| carload | c. l. |
| carriage paid | cge. pd. |
| carried down | c/d |
| carried forward | c/f |
| carried over | c/o |
| carrier's risk | C.R. |
| cartage | ctge. |
| case(s) | c/, c/s |
| cash before delivery | C. B. D. |
| cash book | C/B |
| cash letter | C/L |
| cash on delivery | C. O. D. |
| cash on shipment | c. o. s. |
| cash order | C/O |
| cash with order | c. w. o. |
| cask(s) | ck. |
| cent(s) | c. |
| Central Standard Time | C. S. T. |
| Central Time | C. T. |
| certificate(s) of deposit | c. o. d., C/D |
| certificate of origin | C/O |
| Certified Public Accountant | C. P. A. |
| chapter (law citations) | c. |
| chapter(s) | ch., chap. |
| Chartered Accountant | C. A. |
| check | ck. |
| chief value | c. v. |
| civil | civ. |
| collateral trust | coll. tr., clt. |
| collection and delivery | c. & d. |
| commercial dock | C/D |
| commercial weight | C. W. |
| Commissioner, Commission | Comm. |

| | |
|---|---|
| Committee | Comm. |
| company's risk | C. R. |
| company, county | Co. |
| consignment | C/N, consgt. |
| consular invoice | C. I. |
| cooperative | co-op. |
| copy to | c. c. |
| corporation | Corp. |
| cost and freight | c. & f. |
| cost, assurance and freight | c. a. f. |
| cost, freight and insurance | c. f. i. |
| cost, insurance and freight | c. i. f. |
| craft loss | c/l |
| credit, creditor | cr. |
| credit note | C/N |
| cumulative | cum. |
| cumulative preferred | cu. pf., cum. pref. |
| current | cur. |
| current account | C/a/c |

**D**

| | |
|---|---|
| daily and weekly till forbidden | d. & w. t. f. |
| day letter | DL |
| days after acceptance | d/a |
| days after date | D/d |
| days after sight | D/s |
| dead freight | d. f. |
| dead weight | d. w. |
| dead weight capacity | d. w. c. |
| debenture | deben. |
| debenture rights | db. rts. |
| debit, debtor | dr. |
| debit note | D/N |
| decibel | db. |
| decision | dec. |
| deferred | def. |
| deferreds (cables) | L. C. |
| delivered | dld. |
| delivered at destination | D/D |

| | |
|---|---|
| delivered out of ship | ex ship |
| delivery order | D/O |
| demand draft | D/D |
| demand loan | D/L |
| department | dept. |
| deposit account | D/A |
| deposit certificates | dep. ctfs. |
| deposit receipt | D/R |
| depreciation | depr. |
| deviation clause | D/C |
| diameter | diam., dia. |
| died | ob. |
| direct current | D. C. |
| director | dir. |
| direct port | d. p. |
| discount | dis. |
| dispatch loading only | d. l. o. |
| district | dist. |
| ditto | do. |
| dividend, division | div. |
| division freight agent | D. F. A. |
| dock warrant | D/W |
| documents against payment | D/P |
| dozen | doz. |
| draft | dft. |
| drawback | dbk. |

## E

| | |
|---|---|
| each | ea. |
| Eastern Daylight Savings Time | E. D. T. |
| Eastern Standard Time | E. S. T. |
| editor, edition(s) | ed. |
| editorial note | Ed. Note |
| effective | eff. |
| electric | elec. |
| electrostatic unit | e. s. u. |
| empty | m. t. |
| enclose, enclosed, enclosure | enc. |
| encyclopedia | encycl. |
| end of month | e. o. m. |

| | |
|---|---|
| endorse, endorsement | end. |
| engineer, engine, engraved | eng. |
| equipment | equip. |
| errors and omissions excepted | E. & O. E. |
| errors excepted | e. e. |
| estate, estimated | est. |
| et alii | et al. |
| et cetera | etc. |
| et sequens | et seq. |
| except as otherwise noted | E. A. O. N |
| except as otherwise herein provided | e. o. h. p. |
| exchange bill of lading | Ex. B. L. |
| ex coupon | ex/cp, x-cp. |
| ex dividend | ex div., x-div. |
| executive | exec. |
| executor | exr. |
| executrix | exrx. |
| ex interest | ex int., x-int. |
| ex new | ex-n. |
| ex officio | e. o. |
| express, expenses, export | exp. |
| ex privileges | x-pr. |
| ex rights | ex r., x-rts. |
| extraordinary session | extra. sess. |
| ex warrants | xw |

**F**

| | |
|---|---|
| facsimile | fac. |
| fair average quality | f. a. q. |
| fair average quality of season | f. a. q. s. |
| fast as can | f. a. c. |
| fathom(s) | fm. |
| feet board measure | fbm. |
| feet per minute | f. p. m. |
| feet per second | f. p. s. |
| figure(s) | fig(s). |
| fire risk on freight | f. r. o. f. |
| firm offer | F. O. |
| first class | A-1 |

| | |
|---|---|
| floating policy, fully paid | F. P. |
| folio, following | fol., ff. |
| foreign exchange | F. X. |
| for example (exempli gratia) | e. g. |
| forward | fwd. |
| for your information | F. Y. I. |
| free delivery | f. d. |
| free from alongside, free foreign agency | f. f. a. |
| free of damage | f. o. d. |
| free of income tax, free in truck | f. i. t. |
| free on board | f. o. b. |
| free on field | f. o. f. |
| free on quay | f. o. q. |
| free on rail | f. o. r. |
| free on steamer | f. o. s. |
| free on truck | f. o. t. |
| free overside | F. O. |
| freight | frt. |
| freight and demurrage | f. & d. |
| freight bill | f. b. |
| freight release | F/R |
| fresh water damage | f. w. d. |
| frequency modulation | FM |
| full interest admitted | f. i. a. |
| full terms | f.t. |

## G

| | |
|---|---|
| gallons per minute | g. p. m. |
| general average | G/A |
| general freight agent | G. F. A. |
| general passenger agent | G. P. A. |
| good fair average | g. f. a. |
| good this month | G. T. M. |
| good this week | G. T. W. |
| good till canceled | G. T. C. |
| government | govt. |
| gross | gro. |

| | |
|---|---|
| gross weight | gr. wt. |
| guaranteed | guar. |

## H

| | |
|---|---|
| handkerchief(s) | hdkf. |
| hardware | hdwr. |
| head | hd. |
| held covered | H. C. |
| high water | H. W. |
| high-water mark | H. W. M. |
| high water ordinary spring tide | H. W. O. S. T. |
| hogshead(s) | hhd. |
| hold for money | H. F. M. |
| horsepower | h. p. |
| hour(s) | hr. |
| hypothesis | hyp. |

## I

| | |
|---|---|
| id est | i. e. |
| idem | id. |
| incorporated | Inc. |
| increased value, invoice value | i. v. |
| indicated horsepower | I. H. P. |
| institute, institution | inst. |
| intelligence quotient | I Q |
| interest | int. |
| Internal Revenue Service | I. R. S. |
| International News Service | INS |
| in the same place (ibidem) | ibid. |
| invoice | inv. |
| invoice book, inwards | I. B. I. |
| invoice book, outwards | I. B. O. |
| italics | ital. |

## J

| | |
|---|---|
| joint account | J/A |
| joint stock | jnt. stk. |
| joule | j |
| journal | jour. |

| | |
|---|---|
| Judge, Justice | J. |
| Judge Advocate | J. A. |
| Justice of the Peace | J. P. |
| Justices | J. J. |
| juvenile | juv. |

## K

| | |
|---|---|
| kilocycle(s) | kc. |
| kilovolts | kv. |
| kilowatt(s) | kw. |
| kilowatt-hour(s) | kw.-hr. |
| knocked down | K. D. |
| knot | k. |

## L

| | |
|---|---|
| landing account | L/A |
| landing and delivery | ldg. & dely. |
| large | lge. |
| latitude | lat. |
| Lawyers Edition | L. ED. |
| leakage and breakage | Lkg. & Bkg. |
| leave | lv. |
| less than carload lot | l. c. l. |
| let me see correspondence | L. M. S. C. |
| letter of authority | L/A |
| letter of credit | L/C |
| life insurance policy | L. I. P. |
| light vessel | Lt. V. |
| limited | Ltd. |
| lire | lr. |
| listed | L |
| loading | ldg. |
| loads | lds. |
| loco citato | loc. cit. |
| logarithm | log. |
| longitude | long. |
| long ton | l. t. |
| lower case | l. c. |
| low water | L. W. |

## M

| | |
|---|---|
| Mademoiselle | Mlle. |
| main hatch | M. H. |
| manager | mgr. |
| manufacturer | mfr. |
| manufacturing | mfg. |
| manuscript(s) | ms(s). |
| margin | marg. |
| marginal credit | M/C |
| marine insurance policy | M. I. P. |
| marked capacity | mc. |
| market value | m. v. |
| married, male | m. |
| Master of ceremonies | M. C. |
| mathematics, mathematical | math. |
| maximum | max. |
| maximum capacity | max. cap. |
| mean effective pressure | m. e. p. |
| measurement | mst. |
| megacycle | mc |
| megaton | mt |
| memorandum(s) | memo(s) |
| memorandum of deposit | M/D |
| merchandise | mdse. |
| miles per hour | m. p. h. |
| minimum bill of lading | min. B/L |
| minute(s) | min. |
| miscellaneous | misc. |
| money order | M. O. |
| month(s) | mo. |
| months after date | m/d |
| months after sight | m/s |
| mortgage certificate coupon | mt. ct. cp. |
| mountain | mt. |
| Mountain Standard Time | M. S. T. |
| my account | m/a |

## N

| | |
|---|---|
| national | natl. |
| National Society, New Series | N. S. |

| | |
|---|---|
| nautical | naut. |
| net proceeds | n/p |
| net register | n. r. |
| net tons, new terms | n. t. |
| net weight | nt. wt. |
| new charter | N/C |
| New England, Northeast | N. E. |
| night letter | N. L. |
| night message | N. M. |
| no account | n/a |
| no advice | N/A |
| no date | N. D., n. d. |
| no effects | N/E |
| no funds | n/f |
| no good | N. G. |
| nolle prosequi | nol. pros. |
| no mark | n/m |
| nominal horsepower | N. H. P. |
| nominal standard | nom. std. |
| nominative | nom. |
| non sequitur | non. seq. |
| nonpersonal liability | N. P. L. |
| non prosequitur | non. pros. |
| nonvoting | n. v. |
| no orders | N/O |
| no protest | N. P. |
| no risk | n. r. |
| no risk after discharge | n. r. a. d |
| note well (nota bene) | n. b., N. B. |
| not elsewhere specified | n. e. s. |
| not otherwise enumerated | N. O. E. |
| not otherwise herein provided | N. O. H. P. |
| not otherwise specified | N. O. S. |
| not sufficient funds | N/S, N. S. F. |
| number | No. |

## O

| | |
|---|---|
| ocean and rail | o. & r. |
| obsolete | obs. |
| official interpretation | off. interp. |
| Old English | OE |

| | |
|---|---|
| Old Series | O. S. |
| old terms, on truck | o/t |
| on account of | o/a |
| on demand | o/d |
| one way | o. w. |
| on sample, on sale | O/S |
| open charter, old charter, overcharge | o/c |
| open policy | O. P. |
| opinion | op. |
| order bill of lading | O. B./L, ob/l |
| order of | O/o |
| out of stock | o/s |
| over, short, and damaged | o. s. & d. |
| owner's risk | o. r. |

**P**

| | |
|---|---|
| Pacific Standard Time | P. S. T. |
| Pacific Time | P. T. |
| package | pkg. |
| packed weight | p. w. |
| page | p. |
| pages | pp. |
| pair, price | pr. |
| pamphlet | pam. |
| parcel post | P. P. |
| partial loss | p. l. |
| participating | part. |
| particular average | P/Av. |
| passed, paid | pd. |
| patent | pat. |
| payable on receipt | P. O. R. |
| pay on delivery | P. O. D. |
| pennyweight | pwt. |
| per annum | p. a. |
| percent, post card | p. c. |
| place of the seal | L. S. |
| please exchange | P. X. |
| port dues | P. D. |
| postmaster | P. M. |
| postscript | P. S. |

power of attorney,
    purchasing agent     P/A
preface     pref.
preferred     pfd.
premium     pm.
prepaid     ppd.
price current,
    petty cash     P/C
principal     prin.
private branch exchange     P. B. X.
professional corporation     P. C.
profit and loss     P. & L.
promissory note     P/N
prompt loading     ppt.
protection and indemnity     p. & i.
pro tempore     pro. tem.
proximate     prox.
public address system     PA
public sale     P/S
put and call     P. A. C.

## Q

quality     qlty.
quantity discount agreement     q. d. a
quarter     qr.
question, query     Q.
questions, queries     Q. Q.
quod erat demonstrandum     Q. E. D.
quod vide     q. v.

## R

radio frequency     r. f.
rail and lake     r. & l.
rail and ocean     r. & o.
rail, lake, and rail     r. l. & r.
railroad     R. R.
railway     Ry.
real estate     R. E.
ream, room(s)     rm.
receipt of goods     R. O. G.
received     rcd.

| | |
|---|---|
| referee, reference | ref. |
| refer to acceptor | R/A |
| refer to drawer | R/D |
| refunding | rf., rfg. |
| regarding | re |
| registered, regulation | reg. |
| regular session | reg. sess. |
| reinsurance | R. I. |
| report | rep. |
| residue | res. |
| repondez s'il vous plait | R. S. V. P., r. s. v. p. |
| returned | retd. |
| return of post for orders | R/p |
| return premium | R. P. |
| revenue account | rev. A/C |
| reversed | revd., rev'd |
| reversing | revg. |
| revolutions per minute | r. p. m. |
| revolutions per second | r. p. s. |
| rotation number | rotn. no. |
| running days | r. d. |
| Rural Free Delivery | R. F. D. |

**S**

| | |
|---|---|
| sack(s) | sk. |
| safe arrival | s/a |
| Saint | St. |
| salvage charges | S. C. |
| salvage loss | s. l. |
| secretary | secy., sec. |
| section(s) | sec. |
| seller 7, 10, 15 days to deliver | s7d, s10d, s15d |
| seller's option, shipping order | S. O. |
| shaft horsepower | shp. |
| share agent | sh. |
| shipment | shpt. |
| shipowner's liability | S. O. L. |
| shipper and carrier | s. & c. |

| | |
|---|---|
| shipper's weights, southwest | S. W. |
| shipping and forwarding | S. & F. A. |
| shipping note | S/N |
| sight draft, bill of lading attached | S. D. B. L. |
| signed | sgd. |
| sine die | s. d. |
| sinking fund | S. F. |
| so, thus | sic |
| society | soc. |
| solicitor(s) | sol. |
| Solicitor's Opinion | Sol. Op. |
| special opinion | sp. op. |
| special term | sp. term |
| standard | std. |
| standard wire gauge | S. W. G. |
| statement of billing | S/B |
| station, stamped | sta. |
| station to station | S. to S. |
| statute(s) | stat. |
| steamer, steamship | str., S. S. |
| sterling | stg. |
| stock | stk. |
| stopping in transit | s. i. t. |
| subject to approval | s/a |
| subject to approval no risk | s. a. n. r. |
| superintendent | supt. |
| supplement | supp. |
| supra protest | S. P. |

**T**

| | |
|---|---|
| telegram, telegraph, telephone | tel. |
| telegraphic transfer | T. T. |
| teletypewriter exchange | TWX |
| territory | ty., ter. |
| thousand | M |
| till forbidden | tf., t. f. |
| time deposits | T/D |
| timed wire service | TWS |

| | |
|---|---|
| time loan | T/L |
| tons registered | T. R. |
| total loss only | t. l. o. |
| township | TWP |
| trade expenses | T. E. |
| Traffic Agent | T. A. |
| transfer order | T. O |
| translated, transportation | trans. |
| transpose | tr. |
| treasurer | treas. |
| trial balance | t. b. |
| trust receipt | T/R |

**U**

| | |
|---|---|
| ultimo | ult. |
| ultra high frequency | UHF |
| underwriter | U/w |
| underwriting account | U/A |
| United Parcel Service | UPS |
| United Press | UP |
| university | univ., U. |
| until countermanded | T/C |

**V**

| | |
|---|---|
| valuation clause | V. C. |
| verse, versus | vs. |
| very high frequency | VHF |
| vice versa | v. v. |
| vide | vid. |
| videlicet | viz. |
| video frequency | v. f., V. F. |
| voting | vt. |

**W**

| | |
|---|---|
| warehouse receipt | W. R. |
| warehouse warrant | W/W |
| warranted | w/d |
| water and rail | w. & r. |
| waterproof paper packing | w. p. p. |
| wavelength | w. l. |
| week | wk. |
| weight | wt. |

| | |
|---|---|
| weight and/or measurement | W/M |
| weight guaranteed | w. g. |
| Western District | W. D. |
| when issued | w. i. |
| wholesale | whsle. |
| with warrants | W. W., ww |
| without prejudice | w. p. |

**Y**

| | |
|---|---|
| year, your | yr. |
| yearbook | yb. |

**Z**

| | |
|---|---|
| zone, zero | z. |
| zoology, zoological | zool. |

## 11:5 ASSOCIATIONS, AGENCIES, ORGANIZATIONS

Some abbreviations are so widely used and understood that it is perfectly proper to use them in the body of a letter. Everyone knows, for example, that ASCAP stands for the American Society of Composers, Authors and Publishers, and UNICEF means the United Nations International Children's Emergency Fund. When using common acronyms, there is no need to explain them. Less familiar usages should be spelled out the first time they are used in a letter and abbreviated thereafter.

**A**

| | |
|---|---|
| Advanced Research Projects Agency | ARPA |
| American Association of Retired Persons | AARP |
| American Association of University Women | AAUW |
| American Bankers Association | A. B. A. |
| American Broadcasting Company | ABC |
| American Federal Tax Reports | A. F. T. R. |
| American Federation of Labor and Congress of Industrial Organizations | AFL-CIO |
| American Institute of Banking | AIB |
| American Management Association | AMA |
| American Medical Association | AMA |
| American Red Cross | ARC |

| | |
|---|---|
| American Society for Prevention of Cruelty to Animals | ASPCA |
| American Society of Composers, Authors, and Publishers | ASCAP |
| American Society of Travel Agents | ASTA |
| American Standards Association | ASA |
| American Statistical Association | A. S. A. |
| Associated Press | AP |
| Atomic Energy Commission | AEC |

**B**

| | |
|---|---|
| Board of Review | Bd. of Rev. |
| Board of Tax Appeals | BTA |
| Bureau of Labor Statistics | BLS |

**C**

| | |
|---|---|
| Central Intelligence Agency | CIA, C. I. A. |
| Civil Aeronautics Administration | CAA |
| Civil Aeronautics Board | CAB |
| Civic Service Commission | CSC |
| Collector (Internal Revenue) | Coll. |
| Columbia Broadcasting System | CBS |
| Commissioner of Internal Revenue | CIR |
| Commodity Stabilization Service | CSS |
| Comprehensive Employment and Training Act | CETA |
| Congress of Racial Equality | CORE |
| Cooperative for American Relief Everywhere | CARE |

**D**

| | |
|---|---|
| Daughters of the American Revolution | DAR |
| Dead Letter Office | D. L. O. |
| Democrat | Dem. |
| Development Loan Fund | DLF |

**E**

| | |
|---|---|
| Equal Rights Amendment | ERA |
| European Recovery Program | ERP |

## F

| | |
|---|---|
| Farm Credit Administration | FCA |
| Federal Bureau of Investigation | FBI |
| Federal Communications Commission | FCC |
| Federal Deposit Insurance Corporation | FDIC |
| Federal Housing Administration | FHA |
| Federal Mediation and Conciliation Service | FMCS |
| Federal Power Commission | FPC |
| Federal Register | Fed. Reg. |
| Federal Reserve Board | F. R. B. |
| Federal Reserve System | F. R. S. |
| Federal Security Agency | FSA |
| Federal Trade Commission | FTC |
| Food and Drug Administration | FDA |

## G

| | |
|---|---|
| General Accounting Office | GAO |
| General Assembly | G. A. |
| General Statutes | G. S. |
| Gross National Product | GNP |

## H

| | |
|---|---|
| Health, Education, and Welfare Department | HEW |
| House Bill (state) | H. B. |
| House Bill (federal) | H. R. |
| House Report | H. Rept. (with number) |
| House Resolution | H. Res. (with number) |
| Housing and Home Finance Agency | HHFA |

## M

| | |
|---|---|
| Member of Congress | M. C. |
| Member of Parliament | M. P. |

## N

| | |
|---|---|
| National Academy of Science | N. A. S. |
| National Association for the Advancement of Colored People | NAACP |

| | |
|---|---|
| National Association of Manufacturers | NAM |
| National Broadcasting Company | NBC |
| National Bureau of Standards | NBS |
| National Education Association | N. E. A. |
| National Labor Relations Board | NLRB |
| National Mediation Board | NMB |
| National Office Management Association | NOMA |
| National Office of Vital Statistics | NOVS |
| National Organization for Women | NOW |
| Nonacquiescence (by CIR) | NA |
| North Atlantic Treaty Organization | NATO |

**O**

| | |
|---|---|
| Organization of Petroleum Exporting Countries | OPEC |

**P**

| | |
|---|---|
| Parent-Teacher Association | P. T. A. |
| Patent Office | Pat. Off. |
| Public Health Service | PHS |
| Public Housing Administration | PHA |

**R**

| | |
|---|---|
| Republican | Rep. |
| Rural Electrification Administration | REA |

**S**

| | |
|---|---|
| Securities and Exchange Commission | SEC |
| Senate Report | S. Rept. (with number) |
| Senate Resolution | S. Res. (with number) |
| Small Business Administration | SBA |
| Social Security Administration | SSA |
| Southeast Asia Treaty Organization | S. E. A. T. O. |
| State Senate Bill | S. F. |

**T**

| | |
|---|---|
| Tax Court of the United States | TC |
| Tennessee Valley Authority | TVA |

## U

| | |
|---|---|
| United Nations | UN |
| United Nations International Children's Emergency Fund | UNICEF |
| United Nations Educational, Social, and Cultural Organization | UNESCO |
| United Nations Relief and Rehabilitation Administration | U. N. R. R. A. |
| United Press International | UPI |

## V

| | |
|---|---|
| Veterans Administration | VA |

## W

| | |
|---|---|
| World Health Organization | WHO |

## Y

| | |
|---|---|
| Young Men's Christian Association | YMCA |
| Young Men's Hebrew Association | YMHA |
| Young Women's Christian Association | YWCA |
| Young Women's Hebrew Association | YWHA |

## CONCLUSION

Abbreviations should be kept in their place and used with discretion. They are an occasional convenience that can easily be abused.

# 12. LETTER FORMAT

First impressions are important, and a letter that is uniform in structure and pleasing to the eye makes the reader more receptive to its contents.

## 12:1 ADDRESS AND SALUTATION

The inside address should duplicate the name of the firm you are addressing, according to their letterhead or their listing in the directory.

## 12:1a Address

Abbreviate or spell out such words as **Company, Limited,** and **Incorporated,** to match the firm's official title. A **The** in the title should never be omitted.

Smith Publishing **Co., Inc.**
R. R. Bowker **Company**
Bobley Publishing **Corporation**
**The** Foundation Press, **Inc.**
W. H. Freeman **& Company**

Use figures for all building numbers except **One.** The building number should not be preceded with **#** or **No.,** or a room number.

One Madison Avenue
1124 Broadway
340 Park Avenue, Room 1416

**Never:**

1 Madison Avenue
#1124 Broadway
No. 340 Park Avenue
Room 1416, 340 Park Avenue

Spell out words that stand for street direction—**South**, **North**, **West**, **East**—except when a line is unusually long. Also spell out the names of streets and avenues that are numbered 12 or under.

660 Fifth Avenue
25 West Eighth Street

When figures are used for street names, it is not necessary to add **nd**, **st**, or **th**. You can refer to it as "Forty-Second Street," but you would address a location there as **East** or **West 42 Street**.

Separate the house number from a numerical street name with a space-hyphen-space to avoid confusion.

1234 - 159 Street

Allow two spaces between the name of the state and the zip code number.

Canton, OH      44709

Include the zip code in the letter as well as on the envelope, in order to have it for your records.

When an individual in a company is being addressed, both the individual name and the company name are included. If there is no street address, the city and state may be placed on separate lines.

Mr. Mark Bentley
Parker Publishing Co., Inc.
West Nyack
New York      10994

**Mr.**, **Mrs.**, **Miss**, or **Ms.** precedes the individual's name, even when a business title is used. The name and title are written on the same line when space permits. Otherwise, they are separated into two lines, or the business title is omitted entirely.

Mr. William W. Durrell, President
Crane Duplicating Service, Inc.
Box 487
Barnstable, MA      02630

Mr. Charles E. Spannaus
Vice President in Charge of Sales
St. John Associates, Inc.,
211 West 61 Street
New York, NY    10023

When writing the officer of a company who has several titles, use the title of the higher office, or the office used in the letters which he or she signs.

Miss Judith Helf, Vice President
**or**
Miss Judith Helf, Production Manager
Ahrend Associates, Inc.
64 University Place
New York, NY    10003

The standard form for the address of a letter is at the top, rather than at the foot. It should begin no less than two and no more than twelve spaces below the date line. If the first line is awkwardly long, it should be carried over and indented two spaces.

Automatic Typewritten
    Letters Corporation
151 West 19 Street

## 12:1b Salutation

When no particular individual is addressed, a plural salutation is used.

Gentlemen:
Ladies:
Ladies and Gentlemen:

The salutation is typed two spaces below the inside address, flush with the left-hand margin, two lines below the attention line, if one is used. Follow the salutation with a colon.

In most cases you will be addressing an individual, and you should capitalize the first word, the title and the name.

My dear Mrs. Armonk:
Dear Mr. Babbett:

The only titles that should be abbreviated are **Mr., Mrs., Ms.,** and **Dr.** Even **Doctor** looks better spelled out.

Dear Ms. Carin:
Dear Doctor Dylan:
Dear Professor Entwood:

Never use a business title in a salutation, and never use any title without a surname.

**Right:**

Dear Mr. Fordham:
Dear Professor Graves:
Dear Doctor Holmes:

**Wrong:**

Dear President Fordham:
Dear Professor:
Dear Doctor:

Never use an academic degree following a salutation.

**Right:**

Dear Mr. Jackson:
Dear Dr. Jackson:

**Wrong:**

Dear Mr. Jackson, M.A.:
Dear Dr. Jackson, LL.D.

**Dear Madam** and **Dear Sir** are extremely impersonal salutations. It is preferable to use the addressee's name. A man and a woman may be addressed jointly as **Dear Sir and Madam**, but use their surnames if there is room.

Dear Miss Knight and Mr. Loew:

This is not a circumstance which will occur often, but two women with the same name are addressed as follows:

**Unmarried:** Dear Misses Martin:
**Married:** Dear Mesdames Martin:
**One Married:** Dear Miss Martin and Mrs. Martin

## 12:2 ATTENTION LINE

The attention line is sometimes used when you do not know the initials of the person to whom you are writing. The correct use, however, is to indicate that the letter may be opened, if necessary, by someone other than the person whose name is mentioned. It is typed two spaces below the address and is not underlined.

**Right:**

Norris Corporation
188 Maple Street
Springfield, MA 01105

Attention: Mr. John Owens

Gentlemen:

**or**

Norris Corporation
188 Maple Street
Springfield, MA 01105

Attention: Mr. Owens

Gentlemen:

**Wrong:**

Norris Corporation
188 Maple Street
Springfield, MA 01105

Attention: Mr. Owens

Dear Mr. Owens:

## 12:3 SUBJECT LINE

A subject line following the salutation alerts the recipient to the nature of the letter, and also provides an easy means of filing the copy in the right place. All important words in a subject line are capitalized. The line may be underlined or written in all capital letters, if you prefer. The subject line is never placed before the salutation, as it is part of the body of the letter. It follows the salutation, two places below it, usually flush with the left-hand margin, although it may be centered.

Mr. James F. Prentice
New Haven Bank & Trust Company
190 Main Street
New Haven, CT 06502

Dear Mr. Prentice:

Re: Estate of William Rogers


Mr. James F. Prentice
New Haven Bank & Trust Company
190 Main Street
New Haven, CT 06502

Dear Mr. Prentice:

Re: ESTATE OF WILLIAM ROGERS


Mr. James F. Prentice
New Haven Bank & Trust Company
190 Main Street
New Haven, CT 06502

Dear Mr. Prentice:

Estate of William Rogers


## 12:4 COMPLIMENTARY CLOSES

The complimentary close is typed two spaces beneath the last line of the letter, and a little to the right of the center of the page. In full block letter style, the close is placed flush with the left-hand margin, thus avoiding the problem of keeping the close within the right margin of the letter.

In a two-word close like **Yours sincerely**, only the first word is capitalized. All closes are followed by a comma.

Most firms today use informal complimentary closes when they address their correspondents by name.

### Informal Complimentary Closes

Sincerely,
Sincerely yours,
Yours sincerely,
Very sincerely,

An even friendlier close may be used where there is a closer relationship between addressor and addressee.

### Personal Complimentary Closes

Yours cordially,
Cordially,
Cordially yours,
Most sincerely,

Some businesspeople close their letters even more informally with expressions of good will.

### Expressions of Good Will

With best wishes,
Best wishes,
With best regards,
Best regards,

Closes like **Yours truly** and **Respectfully yours** are used only on very formal occasions, usually when the recipients are addressed as **Sir** or **Madam**, **Ladies** or **Gentlemen**.

### Formal Complimentary Closes

Very truly yours,
Yours very truly,
Yours truly,
Respectfully,
Yours respectfully,
Respectfully yours,
Very respectfully yours,

## 12:5 SIGNATURE AND IDENTIFICATION INITIALS

Type the writer's signature and position four spaces beneath the complimentary close. The business title is typed beneath the name, unless the letter is a purely personal one. If identification initials are used, they appear one space below the last line of the signature, flush with the left margin.

## 12:5a Signature

The firm's name is usually omitted in the signature of a letter, unless it is a formal document. When the firm name is used, it is typed two spaces below the close, and the writer's name appears four spaces below the firm's name. The firm's name should be typed in capitals as it appears on the letterhead. Type signatures exactly as signed by dictators, using initials only where they do.

Cordially,

Very truly yours,
T. TWAIN AND COMPANY


Samuel S. Stone
Vice President

Samuel S. Stone
Vice President

When signing a letter in your own name, as the executive's secretary, precede the executive's name by **Mr.**, **Miss**, **Ms.**, **Mrs.**, or **Dr.**, and omit initials, unless someone else in the firm has the same name.

Sincerely yours,


Secretary to Miss Williams

If you sign your superior's name to a letter, your initials should be placed immediately below.

Yours sincerely,

*Bruce Bliven*

Bruce Bliven        *2ρ*
General Manager

A woman should sign her first name in full, as her surname preceded by initials alone can cause confusion, unless she precedes the initials by (**Mrs.**), (**Miss**), or (**Ms.**).

Your female employer can have her signature typed in any

way that she prefers, but these are the correct forms, according to marital status.

### (1) Divorcee

A divorcee **never** uses her ex-husband's given name. Her typed signature should be either

(Mrs.) Catherine C. Caldwell

or a combination of her maiden name and her former husband's surname:

(Mrs. Coolidge Caldwell)

but, she is no longer entitled to call herself

Mrs. Charles Caldwell.

### (2) Married or Widowed

A married woman or widow may precede her typed signature with (**Mrs.**), or she may type her married name in parentheses beneath the handwritten signature:

(Mrs.) Dorothy Davis
(Mrs. Edward Davis)

Sometimes a married woman prefers to use her maiden name as a signature, followed by her married name in parentheses:

Florence Faber (Gilmore)

She can then be addressed in return as either **Miss Faber** or **Mrs. Gilmore**.

### (3) Single

A female correspondent is presumed to be a **Miss** unless she indicates otherwise, so it is not necessary to put (**Miss**) before the signature. If she wishes to be addressed as **Ms.**, she should so indicate.

## 12:5b Identification Initials

The dictator's and transcriber's initials are usually typed at the bottom of a letter, although there is no real necessity for it. The signer of the letter is obviously the dictator, unless otherwise indicated, and the transcriber's initials mean nothing to the recipient. For reference purposes, the identification initials place responsibility for the letter's contents upon the owners of the initials, and this was probably the original idea.

There are a number of ways in which the initials may be typed, according to company policy or the dictator's preference. Assuming that the dictator's initials are **HAD** and the secretary's are **IJ**, these are the various options.

HAD:ij
HAD/ij
HAD:IJ
HAD/IJ
H. A. Dodge: IJ (when dictator's name is not included in typed signature)
KLM:HAD:IJ (with letter signed by someone other than dictator)
ij (when only the secretary's initials are a matter of record)
IJ

## 12:6 LETTER STYLES, NEW AND OLD

Choice of overall letter format is up to the department head or individual writer, unless there is a definite company ruling in this regard. No one style is intrinsically superior to another, although the various block styles are currently favored.

### 12:6a Block Styles

**Full block** style has date, address, salutation, and signature flush with the left-hand margin. There is no indentation for the start of each paragraph. Open punctuation is used in the address, with no punctuation except the comma separating city and state, or the comma between a name and title on the same line.

**Block** style is modified by putting the date in the upper right-hand corner and the signature and close at bottom right. **Semiblock** style is a further modification, frequently used, in which the address is flush with the left margin, but the first line of each paragraph is indented five or ten spaces.

## Full Block

September 12, 19XX

Mr. George J. Nathan
Osgood Advertising Agency
15 Peachtree Street
Atlanta, GA    30332

Dear Mr. Nathan:

Xxxxxxxxxxxxx xxxxxxxxxxxxxxxx xxxxxxxxxxxxxxxx
xxxxxxxxxxxxxx xxxxxxxxx xxxxxxxxx.

Xxxxxxxxxxxxxxxxx xxxxxxxxxxxxxxxxxxxxxx xxxxxxx
xxxxxxxxxxx xxx xxxxxxxxxxxxx xxxxxxxxx xxxxxxxx
xxxxxxxxxxxxxxxxxx xxxxxxxxxx xxxxxxxxxxxxx xxxxx
xxxxxxxxxxxxxxxxxx xxxxxxxxx xxxxx xxxxxxx xxxxxxxxxxx
xxxxxxxx.

Xxxxxxxxxxxxx xxxxxxxxx xxxxxx xxxxxxxxxxxxx xxxxxxx
xxxxxxxxxx xxxxxxxxxxxxx xxxxxxx xxxxxxxxxxxxxxxx.

Sincerely,


Ruth Stevenson
Advertising Manager

## Block, Modified

September 12, 19XX

Mr. George J. Nathan
Osgood Advertising Agency
15 Peachtree Street
Atlanta, GA    30332

Dear Mr. Nathan:

Xxxxxxxxxxx xxxxxxxx xxxxxx xxxxxxxxxx xxxxxxxxxxx
xxxxxxxxxxxxxx xxxxxxxxxxxxxxx xxxxxxxxxx.

Xxxxxxxxxxxxxxxx xxxxxxxx xxxxxxx xxxxxxxxxx xxxxxxxxx
xx xxxxxxxxxxxxxxxx xxxxxxxxxxxxxxxx xxxxxx xxxxxxxx
xxxxxxx. xxxxxxxxxxxx xxxxxxxxxx xxxxxxx xxxxxxxxxxxxx
xxxxxx xxxxxx xxxxxxxxx xxxxxxxxxxxx xxxxx.

Xxxxxxxxxxxxxxxx xxxxxxxxxxxxxx xxxxxxxxxxx xxxxxxxx
xxxxxx xxxxxxxxxx xxxxxxxxxxxxxxxx.

Sincerely,


Ruth Stevenson
Advertising Manager

**Semiblock**

September 12, 19XX

Mr. George J. Nathan
Osgood Advertising Agency
12 Peachtree Street
Atlanta, GA    30332

Dear Mr. Nathan:

    Xxxxxxxxxxx xxxxxxxxx xxxxxxxxxxxxx xxxxxxxxx xxxxxxxxxxxxxxxxx xxxxxxxx xxxxxxx xxxxxxxxxxxx xxxxxxxxx xxxxxxx.

    Xxxxxxxxx xxxxxxxxxxx xxxxxxxxxxxxxxxxxx xxxxxxx xxxxx xxxxxxxxxxxxxxx xxxxxxxxxxxx xxxxxxxxxxxxxxxx xxxxxxxx xxxx xxxxxxx xxxxxxxxxxxx xxxxxxxxxxxxx xxxxxxxxxxxxxxx xxxxxxxxxxx xxxxx xxxxx.

    Xxxxxxxxxxxxxxxxxx xxxxxxx xxxxxxxxxxxxxxx xxxxxxxxxxxxx xxxx xxxxxxxxxxxxxxxxx.

    Sincerely,

    Ruth Stevenson
    Advertising Manager

**12:6b** Other Styles

The **indented** style uses an address with closed punctuation. Each line is slightly indented from the previous one. The typed signature is also indented three spaces from the close.

The **official** style places the address below the signature, flush with the left-hand margin. Identification initials and enclosure notations are typed two spaces below the last line of the address. This format has a personal feeling, because it starts right out with the salutation.

**Simplified** letter style contains a subject line but omits the salutation and complimentary close. Otherwise, it resembles **full block**. It is used in form letters of various kinds.

## Indented

October 1, 19XX

Mrs. Violet Thompson, Comptroller,
   Underwood Manufacturing Company,
     123 State Street,
      Dallas, TX   79908

Dear Mrs. Thompson:

      Xxxxxx xxxxxxxxxx xxxxxxxxxxxxxxxx xxxxxxxxx
xxxxxxxxxx.

      Xxxxxxxxxxxxxx xxxxxxxxxxxxxx xxxxxxxxxxxxxx
xxxxxxxx xxxxxxxxx xxxxxx xxxxxxxxxxxxxx xxxxxxxxxx
xxxxxxxxxx.

      Xxxxxxxx xxxxxx xxxxxxxxxxxxxx xxxxxxxxx
xxxxxxxxxxxxxx xxxxxx xxxxxxxxxxx.

Sincerely yours,


Walter Young, C.P.A.

## Official

April 15, 19XX

Dear Mr. Young:

      Xxxxxxxxx xxxxxxxxxxxx xxxxxxxxxx xxxxxxxxxx
xxxxxxxxxxxxxxx.

      Xxxxxxxxxx xxxxxxxxxxxxxxxx xxxxxxxxxxxx
xxxxxxxxxxx xxxxxxxxxx xxxxxxxx xxxxxxxxxxxxxx
xxxxxxxxxxx xxxxxxxxxxxxxxxx xxxxxxxxxx xxxxxxxxxx
xxxxxx.

      Xxxxxxxxxx xxxxxxxxxxxxxx xxxxxxxxxxxxxx
xxxxxxxxxx.

Cordially,


Violet Thompson
Comptroller

Mr. Walter Young
Abbott and Young
342 Bingham Avenue
Salt Lake City, Utah   84115

ID
enclosure

(This dropped address could also be used in conjunction with **modified** or **full block** styles.)

**Simplified**

February 19, 19XX

Mr. Bruce Chatham, President
Douglas Machinery Corp.
222 Prospect Street
Portland, Maine      04105

THE COMPUTER AND YOU

Xxxxxxxxxxxxx xxxxxxxxxxxx xxxxxxxxxxxxxxx xxxxxxxxxx
xxxxx xxxxxxxx xxxxxxxxxxxxxxxxxxxxxx xxxxxxxxxxxx
xxxxxxxxxxxxxxxxxxxx.

Xxxxxxxxxxxxxxxxxxx xxxxxxxxxxxxx xxxxxxxxxxxxxxxx
xxxxxxx xxxxxxxxxxxxxxxxx xxxxxxxxxxxxxx xxxxxxxxx
xxxxxxxxxxx xxxxxxxx xxxxxxxxxxxxxxxx.
Xxxxxxxxxxxxxxxxxxxxxxxxxxxx.

Ellis F. Grace
Sales Manager

**12:6c** Speed Messages and Interoffice Memoranda

Speed message forms are widely used to save time when a formal letter is not necessary. They are no substitute for a more detailed letter or personal telephone call, but they fill a need to put something down in writing in order to give a quick answer or obtain a fast written reply. Interoffice memoranda serve the same purpose, but are designed for use within the organization.

**1. Speed Messages**

These forms are ruled so that the message can be written quickly in longhand if desired, with no salutation or close. A **reply message** enables the recipient to respond immediately on the same form.

The **speed messages** are usually set up like this:

SPEED MESSAGE

From
Jason Holmes Co.
217 Eastland Avenue
Detroit, MI      48236
TO _____    (313) 475-5390

_____

SUBJECT _____ DATE _____

_____

_____

_____

_____ Signed _____

---

REPLY MESSAGE

From
Jason Holmes Co.
217 Eastland Avenue
Detroit, MI      48236
TO _____    (313) 475-5390

_____

SUBJECT _____ DATE _____

_____

_____

Please Reply To _____ Signed

_____

_____

_____

DATE _____ Signed _____

Person Addressed Return This Copy to Sender

It is a nice touch to detract from the formality of these messages by preceding the signature with **Best wishes** or **Regards**.

### 2. Interoffice Memoranda

Office memos should be written with as much care as any other letters. They should be routed systematically when going to more than one person, either alphabetically, by location, by rank, or by job priority.

Interoffice or interdivision memos and letters have no salutations or complimentary closes. They can be addressed and signed in either of two ways.

(a)

TO:  Mr. K. Lamson
FROM:  Marian Nolan
SUBJECT: Word Processing System

(body of memorandum)

(b)

Mr. K. Lamson

(body of memorandum)

         Marian Nolan

When the memorandum is going to several recipients, it is addressed as follows, with an extra copy for each addressee:

TO: Mr. K. Lamson
  Mrs. May Pierce
  Miss R. Swart

Sometimes a single copy of a memorandum is to go in succession to each person addressed, in which case it is indicated like this:

1) Mr. K. Lamson
2) Mrs. M. Pierce
3) Miss R. Swart

The name of the person writing the memo may be included as number 4, so that the memorandum will be returned to the sender.

The letters **F. Y. I.** (for your information) are put after the names of persons to whom copies are being sent merely to keep them informed.

## CONCLUSION

Letter format is second nature to the experienced secretary, but an occasional review will refresh your memory and keep you from becoming lax.

## FINAL WORD

Today's secretary is more than a mechanism for transcribing someone else's words. The modern secretary is an articulate member of a management team, whose knowledge of correct English is an invaluable asset.

## CHART V: MOST USED FORMS OF ADDRESS

### Company Official

Mr. William Grant,
  President
P.S. Mencken Corporation
(local address)
Dear Mr. Grant:

Mrs. Elizabeth Meade,
  President
Sears and Ward Company
(local address)
Dear Mrs. Meade:

### Doctor

Lawrence Langer, M.D.
(local address)
Dear Dr. Langer:

Katherine Karlin, D.D.S.
(local address)
Dear Dr. Karlin:

### Lawyer

Mr. David Erikson
Attorney at Law
(local address)
Dear Mr. Erikson:

Miss Dorothy Evans
Attorney at Law
(local address)
Dear Miss Evans:

### Mayor

Honorable Herbert Vielehr
Mayor of the City of
  New York
(local address)
Dear Mayor Vielehr:

Honorable Helen Wills
Mayor of the City of
  Hartford
(local address)
Dear Mayor Wills:

### Professor

Professor Frank Oldenberg
(local address)
Dear Professor Oldenberg:

Grace C. Perkins, Ph.D.
(local address)
Dear Dr. Perkins:

## Cleric

The Reverend Lawrence
  Wylie
(local address)

The Reverend Victoria
  Benson, D.D.
(local address)

Dear Father Wylie

Dear Dr. Benson:

Rabbi Morris Loeb
(local address)

Dear Rabbi Loeb:

## CHART VI: COMMON ABBREVIATIONS

| | |
|---|---|
| ABC | American Broadcasting Company |
| AFL-CIO | American Federation of Labor and Congress of Industrial Organizations |
| AMA | American Medical Association |
| AP | Associated Press |
| ASCAP | American Society of Composers, Authors, and Publishers |
| CBS | Columbia Broadcasting System |
| DAR | Daughters of the American Revolution |
| ERA | Equal Rights Amendment |
| FBI | Federal Bureau of Investigation |
| GNP | Gross National Product |
| HEW | Health, Education, and Welfare Department |
| I.N.S. | International News Service |
| NAACP | National Association for the Advancement of Colored People |
| N.A.M. | National Association of Manufacturers |
| NBC | National Broadcasting Company |
| N.E.A. | National Education Association |
| NOW | National Organization for Women |
| NSA | National Secretaries Association |
| OPEC | Organization of Petroleum Exporting Countries |
| PTA | Parent-Teacher Association |
| REA | Rural Electrification Administration |
| SEC | Securities and Exchange Commission |
| UNESCO | United Nations Educational, Social, and Cultural Organization |
| UNICEF | United Nations International Children's Emergency Fund |
| UPI | United Press International |
| YMCA | Young Men's Christian Association |
| YWCA | Young Women's Christian Association |
| YMHA | Young Men's Hebrew Association |
| YWHA | Young Women's Hebrew Association |

# Index